W0232710

HUMAN
AT WORK

ADVANCE PRAISE FOR THE BOOK

'Richard's insightful book walks the reader through the most pertinent aspects of the workplace today. The principles and guidance laid out so clearly in this book will no doubt prove invaluable to readers across the spectrum. Taking a pragmatic and lucid approach to highlight and tackle issues that plague most members of the corporate world, Richard has distilled key lessons from his own experience. This essential piece provides a path to thriving in the modern workplace'—Anand Mahindra, chairman, Mahindra Group

'I have known Richard Lobo for thirty years now. He is approachable, empathetic, kind, friendly, team-oriented and a good listener. Most importantly, he always thought of new ideas to make human talent at Infosys aspirational, curious, innovative, productive, happy and identify with the company goals. In this book, he brings these unique attributes, in his unique way, to help us cope with today's fast-changing world'—N.R. Narayana Murthy, founder, Infosys

'We are in a world where a combination of the way we work and technology will drive employment and growth. This book shows how the human–machine frontier is changing, with businesses introducing automation and technology at an accelerated pace and the human at the workplace needing to adapt at a never-before-experienced speed. Richard explores how jobs and skills will evolve, and how each of us must adapt to leverage human skills of intuition and reasoning to remain relevant and useful'—Omkar Goswami, economist

'In an era marked by rapid changes to the way we approach business, this book delivers a compelling vision for how the future of work will look like in a world that is going to see multiple shifts in technology and human behaviour. The world we inhabit today is filled with promise but also challenges. I have known Richard over the years, and his observation and perspective on the human dimension of work has been thought-provoking and useful. Through this book, he presents to the reader a path to approach the new world of work where the human and the machine will come together to augment capabilities towards a more creative future'—K.V. Kamath, former CEO and MD, ICICI Bank

'India's journey towards becoming a global powerhouse depends on its human capital—the driving force behind sustainable economic growth and innovation. This book focuses on uniting technological advances with

human perspectives to create sustained competitive advantage for the enterprise while making work more fulfilling for the individual. In an era of AI, humanoids, quantum computing, etc., where the speed of change is very high, the nature of work will change rapidly, and enterprises and individuals need to understand and prepare to meet this very rapid change. Richard Lobo is living this change as a global human resource leader and his book should be a must-read for all interested in human capital'
—T.V. Mohandas Pai, chairman, Aarin Capital Partners

'In a world where technology and globalization are rapidly reshaping the workforce, *Human at Work* offers a comprehensive guide to understanding and thriving in the evolving work environment. This insightful book explores key trends and transformations that are defining the future of work, from the rise of remote and gig economies to the integration of artificial intelligence and automation. More interestingly, it helps the reader to re-examine their own approach to work. Whether you are an executive, entrepreneur or professional seeking to future-proof your career, this book provides the tools and insights needed to navigate the complexities of the modern workplace in a human-centric way'—Anish Shah, CEO, Mahindra Group

'I found *Human at Work* insightful reading for anyone looking to explore the innovations driving the future and their implications on our way of working. Richard has brought his deep expertise in working with people and technology to help the reader understand the challenges that every knowledge worker will face in the next decade. He presents us a compelling case to look at our everyday work life with a future-proof lens. Whether you are an early career professional or an experienced manager, I would highly recommend this book as a guide to navigating the future in a way that will help you thrive in an ever-evolving world'
—Meher Pudumjee, chairperson, Thermax

'As the impact of technology on work and workplaces continues to evolve at a rapid pace, *Human at Work* provides a useful examination of how these advancements are set to redefine our professional and personal lives. This thought-provoking book uncovers the transformative power of the human and machine coming together. Using his experience across industries and functions, Richard illuminates the challenges and opportunities that lie ahead, offering practical advice on how each one of us can adapt to the emerging world of work. This book is recommended reading for business professionals and anyone interested in the future of work'—Mohit Joshi, CEO, Tech Mahindra

'With expert analysis and practical advice, this book addresses crucial questions facing employers and employees alike: How can businesses adapt to stay competitive? What skills will be essential in the new economy? How can workers safeguard their careers against disruption? *Human at Work* is your essential road map to understanding the challenges and opportunities that lie ahead. I have known Richard for a long time and have always appreciated his ability to take a holistic perspective, bring in deep professional insights and facilitate and navigate change, effortlessly. Through this book, he brings forth his keen observations to help the reader understand change, adapt and step into the future with confidence and clarity, ready to make the most of the new world of work'—Anil Verma, CEO, Godrej & Boyce

HUMAN AT WORK

Arm yourself to thrive in a fast-changing workplace

RICHARD LOBO

PENGUIN
BUSINESS

An imprint of Penguin Random House

PENGUIN BUSINESS

Penguin Business is an imprint of the Penguin Random House group of companies whose addresses can be found at global.penguinrandomhouse.com

Published by Penguin Random House India Pvt. Ltd
4th Floor, Capital Tower 1, MG Road,
Gurugram 122 002, Haryana, India

Penguin Random House India

First published in Penguin Business by Penguin Random House India 2024

Copyright © Richard Lobo 2024

All rights reserved

10 9 8 7 6 5 4 3 2 1

The views and opinions expressed in this book are the author's own and the facts are as reported by him which have been verified to the extent possible, and the publishers are not in any way liable for the same.

Please note that no part of this book may be used or reproduced in any manner for the purpose of training artificial intelligence technologies or systems.

ISBN 9780143466345

Typeset in Sabon by MAP Systems, Bengaluru, India
Printed at Thomson Press India Ltd, New Delhi

This book is sold subject to the condition that it shall not, by way of trade or otherwise, be lent, resold, hired out, or otherwise circulated without the publisher's prior consent in any form of binding or cover other than that in which it is published and without a similar condition including this condition being imposed on the subsequent purchaser.

www.penguin.co.in

FSC www.fsc.org MIX Paper | Supporting responsible forestry FSC® C010615

Dedicated to the people I have worked with over the years.
The intersection of our paths has helped shape this book

Contents

Introduction xi

1. Is the Robot Applying for My Job? 1
2. Painting a Masterpiece While Clearing Your Mail 24
3. Dr Jekyll and Mr Manager 43
4. Embracing Tomorrow: Rediscovering Health for a Fulfilling Life 66
5. Crafting Human Experiences at Work 87
6. Imagining Your Office of the Future 109
7. Failing Successfully 130
8. Playing the Long Game 149
9. Doing the Right Things Right 171

Epilogue 191
Acknowledgements 195
Notes 197

Introduction

In the 1985 Hollywood sci-fi movie *Back to the Future*, small-town California teen Marty McFly finds himself stuck in the 1950s when an experiment by his eccentric scientist friend Doc Brown goes awry. Travelling through time in a modified DeLorean car, Marty encounters a world very different from what he knows. Similarly, if office workers of today got sent back to the 1970s, a time when one of the biggest office complexes, the twin-towers at the World Trade Center in New York City, were up and running, they would be perplexed with what they saw in terms of equipment, processes and ways of working.

What if we were to travel fifty years ahead to an office in 2070? Would we understand what we encounter in the future office, and more importantly, would we be able to navigate and perform in the new world of work?

Today, some of us may have a fifty-year career span if we start working at the age of twenty. If we are going to be part of the work world for this duration, we need to prepare ourselves for the shifts we will encounter. Over five decades, the world of work will change dramatically, and each of us will have to adapt ourselves to change. Otherwise, we will find the place the way Marty did—unfamiliar and difficult.

Every journey to the future starts with imagining what we might encounter and preparing ourselves for it. This book is written with the objective of spurring you to think about the various dimensions of the world of work and how you might take actions today to make yourself ready for tomorrow.

Charles Dickens was not referring to the office when he opened his 1859 novel, *A Tale of Two Cities*, with the line, 'It was the best of times, it was the worst of times', but it fits in perfectly with what we see happening around us. While our world of work is exciting and challenging, many times it's a struggle to keep pace with what is happening. On the one hand, we have an infusion of innovative technology that makes us more productive. We also see new work models and ways of working, better user experiences as employees and more avenues to learn and develop skills. On the other hand, we have stress points due to world events, such as conflict and climate change, inward-looking governments, concerns around workplace wellness and other challenges to navigate. To have a successful and fulfilling career, the human at work will need to balance these shifts.

Human endeavour, specifically that in the form of organized labour, has seen shifts in its form and methods due to changes in technology, customer demands and worker preferences. In 1712, the invention of the steam engine saw a shift of work from the home workshops of individual artisans to factories where a group of people could work together. This model was more commercially viable, allowing for the introduction of machinery beyond the individual craftsman's purchasing power. The 1950s saw the factory model being replicated for office workers with large offices being opened in cities and workers commuting to their place of work. In many ways, these offices mirrored factories with office tools like typewriters and workflows that moved work from table to table, like a conveyor belt.

The entry of the computer and advancements in communication technology resulted in an increase in knowledge workers, and soon companies could have offices across cities, i.e., networked offices linked by communication technology. However, the original factory model of the industrial age, in which large groups of people commuted to a place of work, remained. In 2020, the Covid-19 pandemic globally brought in what can be termed the fastest change to our world of work, where we went from working in an office to working from our homes in a period of two weeks. Simultaneously, we saw the entry of new technologies like artificial intelligence (AI), better network and computing power, new collaboration tools, etc., which allowed us to work seamlessly in a way that our exact location, whether at home, in office or a park, did not matter. We are now at an inflection point where we can change our way of working for the better by applying thought to make our work better, more human, efficient and fulfilling.

It's understandable that there is tremendous excitement as well as apprehension about the new world of work that we see evolving right before us. There has been a large disruption to both the way we work in terms of our work rhythms: morning commute, midafternoon breaks, post-work socials, business travel, meetings, etc., as well as the kind of work we do—fixed outcome measures, task and time-based, static goals, annual appraisals, etc. This disruptive change is due to two main reasons: the entry of transformative technology into the workplace and a change in approach by companies on how to capture and trade the commercial value of human effort. To offer an example, today, ride-sharing companies do not own any cars, yet they combine technological innovation and human effort to package and sell a service to the consumer in a seamless manner. In the future, it's possible that companies won't employ people. They will put out work packets that workers around the world could bid for, deliver and get paid for without ever needing to be employed. The company's work automation system will then stitch the work packets together into a final product ready for review.

We are experiencing probably the biggest change to the way of working since the beginning of the industrial revolution, almost 250 years ago. Many workers protested the introduction of new working methods in the nineteenth century, but others learned to use these methods to become better and more productive. Just as some of the successful early workers of the industrial age emerged from a set of skilled craftsmen in their home workshops, the new world of work will be hungry for the modern office worker who adapts and manages this change using creativity, intelligence and shared learning.

In his book, *On the Origin of Species*, Charles Darwin speaks about evolutionary adaptation. He wrote this book based on his travels in 1837 to study new worlds and their inhabitants. His observation was that it is not the most intellectual or strongest of the species that survives, but the one that is best able to adapt and adjust to the changing environment in which it finds itself. In the same way, for us to adapt and make the present the best of times of our career, we need to adapt, learn and most importantly, navigate the ambiguous. The world of work is witnessing multiple shifts that will need us to adapt—a change in workplace demographics as younger workers replace those who are older; the emergence of new technologies that will replace human labour; geopolitical happenings that will constrain free deployment of labour and a change in living conditions with many places in the world seeing climate disruptions. The creatures Darwin observed evolved over time; in our case, as Marty finds in the movie, we must adapt much faster.

During an interaction with students at a business school, I realized that many of the questions they had for me were about navigating the future of work. There was curiosity about the future as well as a deep intent to build a successful career. A few students seemed eager to continue the interaction over tea, and one of them remarked that it would benefit if some of the answers I gave them were made available for a larger audience.

This book is based on my three decades of experience in diverse organizations, during which the world of work has dramatically changed. The focus is on helping the reader adapt to and thrive in the new world of work by learning to balance the human skills that are essential at work with the changes brought about by technology and business models. It draws on learnings and observations from years of successful managerial practice. The techniques and methods used cover the areas of managing people, leading and motivating teams, acquiring and skilling talent, assessing and rewarding performance, etc. The idea is that the possibilities offered by technologies like AI, augmented reality, data analytics, predictive modelling, deep learning, etc. can be used to incorporate and improve the aforementioned human skills for us to do better as early adaptors.

In 1960, the term 'cyborg' was introduced in a story to indicate an entity made up of both biological and artificial technology elements. The cyborg had abilities beyond those exhibited by either its biological or technological parts alone, and this amplified its potential. Stories depict how cyborgs have mental and/or physical capabilities that are far beyond those of humans. Similarly, we can improve our human capabilities with the intelligent use of technology to become exponentially better at work and beyond. We can aim to be better not only in terms of productivity and the value we add, but also in terms of how to become happier, healthier and fulfilled with what we do at work and beyond.

Habits are a big part of our lives. Research[1] has shown that about half the activities we perform daily are repeated in the same way. Habits help us deal with the complexity we face in the world. They help us save time in an ambiguous situation. Do you recall ordering a familiar dish in a restaurant when faced with multiple choices? Many of our work processes and work habits are the result of many years of learning. For example, when electronic mail became possible, we replicated some of our old habits for handling physical mail. We opened the mail that had important information and ignored the junk. When the pandemic made us go remote, we quickly used available technology to replicate our physical workspaces in remote mode. We met in virtual meeting rooms, and some offices even had 'virtual' water cooler rooms to recreate discussions that people had near water coolers or break rooms. We still assess people's performance based on output and then slot them into categories using a method that was first perfected for measuring the quality of machined parts in a factory. Change doesn't happen fast, and it's certainly not easy to get rid of old habits, but we cannot adapt to change unless we consciously break the habits that have become irrelevant.

Abraham Lincoln was the first to point out that the best way to predict the future is to create it. We may not be involved in inventing machines or business models that change the future of our work, but we can certainly join in creating the future that these machines make possible. If we take inventions that have disrupted work life, starting from the spinning jenny to the introduction of ChatGPT, the benefits have come more from the right usage of the invention than from the innovation itself. Creating innovative uses is what will eventually make us more productive and our lives better. In that pursuit, learning and unlearning are needed. Some of us take bets quicker than others and while not all bets work out for the better, failure is very much a part of success when it comes to adaptation.

This book is about using imagination to create a better future of work by channelling the fruits of technological innovation along with a human-centred approach to deployment. We cannot expect to get better by doing the same things; we need to do different things altogether. By exploring details of both human skills that matter at work as well as technology that can help, the book aims to help the reader be future-ready.

In the chapters that follow, we will explore both human skills and technology adaptation at the individual and enterprise levels. It's expected that readers will play multiple roles over the course of their career and will want to leverage the learnings, both for themselves and for their team and company. We will use the concept of micro-transformation to overcome the sluggishness that confronts individuals and companies when they embark on change. Towards this purpose, there are exercises, included wherever appropriate, so that ideas can be actioned quickly at a micro level. The examples used to illustrate concepts and use cases provided are simple and can be used in multiple contexts. The book is primarily designed to be a guide for someone at the early stage of their career, yet aspiring to be a future leader in their organization. However, the book can also be used by an experienced manager who is looking for ideas to lead their team better and to improve their way of working.

The chapters cover topics that are relevant to the modern worker and workplace. While each chapter independently explores a topic of interest, the chapters are connected in a logical sequence that will cover the overarching theme of the human at work in the new world of work. Most chapters have relevant organizational case studies, examples and tools that can be used to practice the learning at the individual and team levels. It is not necessary for the chapters to be read in the sequence in which they appear. You could choose relevant chapters based on your current area of interest and return to the others as needed.

The world of work is going to be disrupted, whichever way we look at it. This book is an attempt to put into perspective some of the changes that will impact our future. By being better informed, we can be better prepared and then work towards taking advantage of the developments that are in store. Without a doubt, the future is going to be interesting and exciting for all of us. For workers of the future, their ability to adapt their skills to the changing needs of the workplace will be critical. This book is not about saying to people, 'You need to adapt' but about helping them understand the change in the context of the present workplace and learn how to build a plan to meet the workplace of tomorrow. Managing change may be a long and painful process, but most of it is an inside job, starting with ourselves. Let's explore this world together.

Chapter 1

Is the Robot Applying for My Job?

I skate to where the puck is going to be, not where it has been.

—Wayne Gretzky

Richie Rich is a fictional character in the Harvey Comics universe. Known as 'the poor little rich boy', he is the only child of fantastically rich parents and has everything one could want. One of the characters in the Richie Rich comic book series is Irona, Richie's robot maid. Irona has human intelligence, including emotional intelligence and is physically stronger than any human. She is able to come to the rescue of humans at any sign of trouble and helps them get out of tricky situations.

Over the last fifty years, a variety of fiction has shaped our imagination of intelligent non-human beings. Our imagination has outpaced reality long before our technology could produce anything remotely similar to what was depicted in our comics, books and movies. The 1920 play *Rossum's Universal Robots* first gave us the term 'robot' to depict a non-human intelligent being, and our imagination has grown since that first seeding. While some of the depictions have been negative and have pictured intelligent robots as hostile to their creators, others have been generally benign and helpful to humans. For the sake of simplicity, we will use the words robots and AI interchangeably in this chapter.

While work on AI has been happening in many places over the years, there have been occasional spurts in its development that have caught our attention because they seemed significant. In 1997, an IBM supercomputer called Deep Blue defeated reigning world champion Gary Kasparov in a game of chess for the first time. Chess was long considered a high-level demonstration of human intelligence, requiring thinking, planning and reasoning. For the first time, artificial intelligence had beaten human intelligence in what was considered a human preserve.

Towards the start of the millennium, many smart innovations competed for attention, including the newly launched iPhone. These innovations demonstrated that near-human artificial intelligence would soon be common, though not in the form of a superhuman maid. In 2016, the AlphaGo program developed by Google DeepMind defeated a top Go player Lee Sedol. Go is an abstract board game that tests the strategic abilities of the two players facing across the board. Invented in China more than 4500 years ago, Go was considered a more difficult programming challenge than chess, as it involved creativity, intuition and strategic thinking. With this demonstration, it was clear that in narrowly defined fields, artificial intelligence could do better than humans.

The next spurt in AI development was seen with the launch of ChatGPT in 2022. For the first time, ordinary users could experience technology that seemed almost human and capable of interacting with the user in a way they would interact with other humans. You could converse with ChatGPT, ask for opinions on complex subjects, engage in work activities and make it do your homework. Within a year of its launch, ChatGPT had become the fastest-growing consumer software application, gaining over 1 million users in less than a week from its launch. Since its applications provide more use to humans besides games, its usage has spread widely, and currently sees more than 1.5 billion visits a month (September 2023).

ChatGPT is based on a technology called generative artificial intelligence, or generative AI. This technology generates text, images, songs and stories by learning patterns and structure from a vast amount of data inputs and then using the learning from these inputs to generate new data that has similar characteristics. Generative AI has the potential to disrupt our world of work, mostly for the better. This technology can help us work better by augmenting our human capabilities. By harnessing its power, we could be more productive, creative and collaborative. As we introduce AI technologies into the workplace, many of our jobs will change. Just like the computer and the smart phone made us better at work, this is another change that will enhance our capabilities.

In about 100 years from the time the robot first appeared in the movies, it seems to have reached a level in terms of capabilities and intelligence to replace its human creators in some of the jobs that till now seemed their exclusive preserve. Let's look at three such jobs to give us an idea of the possibilities of robots aiding humans.

Over the last fifty years, automation has changed many things a pilot has to do to control an aircraft. In fact, the cockpits of modern aircraft like the A350 bear little resemblance to the cockpits five decades prior. The aircraft autopilot system incorporates a significant amount of automation, enabling it to operate autonomously under human supervision. In its most modern offering, the A350 model, Airbus worked on improving the autopilot to extend the plane's automation capabilities even further. The project, codenamed 'Dragonfly', focused on three main phases: automatic landing, taxi assistance and emergency diversion in case the pilot is incapacitated for some reason. While the first two phases had already been under some kind of development for a while, the third one is new and interesting. Airbus conducted testing of an automatic emergency descent system. The design of this technology allows it to fully replace the pilots and land the aircraft at the nearest usable airport, performing all tasks that a human would typically perform. Under automatic control, the plane can interact with air traffic control, descend and land while considering air traffic, weather, terrain and other factors that are relevant for landing safely.

The automatic pilot technology processes information in real time and makes the decision on where and how to land safely. It uses a combination of normal cameras, infrared sensors and radar. It also uses a synthetic artificial voice for communicating with air traffic control. Airbus does state that while there are no plans to remove humans from the cockpit, they will continue to work on further automation and in a few years, we could be seeing only one pilot in the cockpit and the other one would be artificial.

The second example is not as complex but equally interesting. In the late 1970s, the telephone had reached a level of penetration that businesses started to use regularly to interact with their customers. It first started as a sales tool, where agents would call customers to sell them a product or service. These agents operated out of a facility that was 'imaginatively' called the call centre. Later, these call centres also started to be used to address customer issues and provide solutions. As this method of solving issues grew in popularity, cheaper labour costs and the easy availability of the internet saw businesses shifting these call centres to countries like India and the Philippines. Over time, these call centres employed thousands of people around the world.

AI can easily be deployed in a call centre, and companies started looking at improving service levels and reducing costs through the deployment of automation. Conversational AI can relieve agents of routine tasks like logging information, generating sales leads, planning call times, retrieving data, answering emails, finding solutions to problems and so on. The agents can only focus on complex interactions that need human intervention, but it is clear that the need for agents will reduce further.[1] Companies realized that the deployment of automation ensures consistency in the customer experience, and the service can be made available 24x7. Moreover, companies can design the system to offer valuable insight that enhance other aspects of their business, such as product design or manufacturing.

The third example illustrates the use of machines for repair and healing. It's a universal truth that no one likes hospitals, and we are even less fond of surgery. In fact, most of us dread even entering the surgical clinic. However, sometimes surgery is the only option to heal what ails us, and we have no choice but to bear it. Surgery usually comes with a long convalescence period and related complications. Most surgical procedures involve a surgeon accessing inner organs with handheld instruments through a large incision, performing whatever fix is needed, suturing the incision and then giving it time to heal.

Today, many surgical procedures are available through what is described as minimally invasive surgery that is assisted or fully performed by a robot. Developments in automation have given surgeons the added benefits of technology that can extend their capabilities while reducing pain and discomfort for patients.

Doctors have been using tools to enhance their capabilities over time. From the early X-ray machines to the modern MRI and PET scanners, imaging has improved to a stage where doctors can see inside a body. Robotic surgery allows doctors to perform complex surgical procedures with more flexibility, precision and control than open surgery allows. For example, a robotic arm can rotate a full 360 degrees to perform a procedure, while a surgeon's wrist cannot. Most surgical robots have cameras and mechanical arms attached to surgical instruments. The surgeon controls the arm while seated at a computer console near the operating table. The surgeon sees a magnified, high-definition 3D image of the surgical site. Current surgical robots also have the capability of doing complex surgeries on their own without human involvement, though they are not allowed to do so due to a lack of confidence from patients as well as regulations to protect the patients.

The surgeons' feedback on these robot surgical systems is positive. They say that the system enhances precision, flexibility and control during the procedure compared to traditional techniques. The patient benefits from shorter recovery times because the incision required is small and blood loss is minimal.

From the cockpit to the call centre to the surgical table, automation has changed the way humans work.

You could potentially replace these professions with others and find similar changes to the way of working. The robot has come to a stage where it can take away some jobs.

But Will the Robot be Interested in Taking Over My Job?

In 2024, there will be more than 2500 passenger airplanes[2] on order by airlines around the world. Customer care centres around the world are seeing an increase in call volumes and are finding it difficult to staff positions. The National Health Service (NHS) in the UK is seeing a median wait time of fourteen-and-a-half weeks.[3] Robots do not seem to be replacing humans in any of the three examples we covered.

A 2020 report from the World Economic Forum[4] states something interesting: while 85 million jobs may be lost by 2025, about 97 million new jobs will emerge. So, what we must worry is not about the robot taking away our current job, but about how we can remain relevant and useful without necessarily being tied to the requirements of our current job.

To understand this better, let's look at how technology works at the interface of the human and the office. If you walk into any office environment, you will see technology deployed for a variety of activities. The office you visit might have an automated entry system or it might be using AI-based virtual office assistants. Using technology, organizations have been able to improve the productivity and efficiency of employees while also bringing in the benefits of better work–life balance and experience. Employees can now focus on more important tasks and spend more time with fellow workers on core activities. The rise of AI and the benefits it brings are another chapter in the office's progress.

Generative AI has been in development for a while and will continue to get better. It is built on what is known as a foundation model. In simple terms, this means training the AI system with large amounts of data, including text and images, so that it slowly starts to recognize patterns in the data and make inferences and predictions. Once it has reached a certain level in terms of learning, the system is fine-tuned for accuracy using more precise data sets. To give an example, think of creating an AI model to recognize a shark when presented with an image containing different ocean creatures. The model is first trained on all the information about the living and non-living things in the ocean. Then the model is fine-tuned by showing it a variety of sharks until it can pick out a shark from any image shown to it. The best part is that the model improves with increased use and interactive learning. The initial training phase is time-consuming and intensive, but after the machine is trained, the benefits are exponential.

Interestingly, early AI inventors worked on mirroring how the human brain worked. The brain is the most powerful computational engine even today, and many machine learning techniques come from the way our brains operate. The billions of neurons in our brains form a network, facilitating our learning and thought processes. The scientists who worked on artificial intelligence have tried to mirror the networks in our brains to build on foundational models to give us deep learning machines that are close to human intelligence. Today, we can have machines process large and unstructured data to perform several activities that were once in the domain of humans—

answer questions, make meaningful inferences, suggest actions, interpret images, guide vehicles safely and so on.

Soon, many office tasks that have been so far performed by humans will be fed into machines, who, over time, will learn to first duplicate and then improve these tasks as they learn. As a human, the advantage you have is that you can keep ahead of the machine, as your brain is at a level of sophistication that is difficult to replicate in a machine. You cannot compete with the machine by doing the jobs of the past, but you can be ahead in the jobs of the future.

Office workers can segregate their work in an office environment using multiple dimensions such as skill, complexity, interface, value, etc. To exemplify this, let's categorize the jobs performed at a hotel using the dimension of complexity. At Level 1 of complexity, we have what are known as interface jobs that involve processing routine transactions like check-in or answering queries from customers and providing a resolution. At Level 2, you have jobs that require an added dimension of decision-making. For example, if you are a frequent guest or member of a hotel chain and the room you booked is not available, you will need some assistance to resolve this. The front desk will probably call a supervisor, who will then make a decision that could either get you an upgrade or a drink voucher that you can use while you wait for your room.

At Level 3, you have ambiguous situations that require judgement and decision-making based on experience. For example, the hotel might want to increase the room tariff, knowing that a large convention is scheduled to take place in the city. This is a judgement call, as increasing the tariff by too much would annoy potential guests, yet keeping the hike low would mean losing some profits.

In the past, a hotel employee would start at a Level 1 job, then get promoted to the role of supervisor and eventually move to becoming a general manager. Technology has now altered the skill set required at each level. Let's see how.

At all three levels, technology can benefit us in different ways. At Level 1, technology can eliminate the need for a front desk, as some hotels have already done in the past.[5] On arrival, you could swipe in your credit card at a kiosk and receive your key from the machine. Present your key to the machine at the time of leaving and you would be checked out automatically. However, people don't normally like checking into a hotel where they deal only with machines. Eliminating the job doesn't mean eliminating humans. Hotels have realized that while technology replaces humans in some ways, it still needs them. The person manning the front desk still appears and has a chat with you, but the skills required have changed. What are the new skills required? The ability to speak multiple languages, engage in meaningful conversations, suggest activities, cross-sell some packages and most importantly, bring in the human element to the interaction that will make the guest want to come back to the hotel. The job has in fact been split; the machine has taken over the uninteresting part and the human is handling the interesting one.

At Level 2, the supervisor could be supplied with guest profiles and pertinent information based on their previous stays and create a suggested list of actions they could take without needing to make the guest wait. For example, if the guest is a business visitor, an offer of a chance to refresh in an available room and a taxi ride to a business meeting would be more useful than a voucher at the bar. The supervisor could instruct the Level 1 worker at the front desk in advance, avoiding any unforeseen requests or problems that would require the supervisor's assistance.

At Level 3, the system could intelligently analyse the data available from previous events to present a 'what if' analysis on room rates. The general manager could then use these inputs to price the rooms in a range that appears reasonable and does not leave the guests with a feeling of being cheated, while at the same time optimizing the revenue for the hotel. The judgement of the human would still be very vital in deciding the final pricing, as only someone with ample experience can make the right call in this situation.

We can see that at all three levels—front desk, supervisor and general managers—the deployment of technology has enabled them to move to a higher level in their jobs and allowed them to learn new skills to make them more productive.

This can be employed in other businesses, such as airlines, supermarket chains, professional service firms and so on. It is clear that technology can enhance operations by automating menial tasks and allowing humans to focus on quality work and decision-making, no matter the industry or the job level.

Humans are better at making decisions involving ambiguity. Ambiguous situations require decision-making based on intuition, and humans are good at this. Machines are far superior at making decisions that require deductions involving data and logic, especially data of considerable volume. Merging the two capabilities of machines and humans makes for a powerful outcome.

Organizations routinely entrust humans with decision-making responsibilities in situations of varying complexity. Those who are better at decision-making progress faster in their careers and eventually become supervisors and managers. Having support from machines will enable more people to move up and improve their earning potential.

In the future, the role of the manager will evolve to work along with the machine. The manager will be more of a question framer—asking the right questions based on the situation, framing the problem and then using machines to help her solve the problem. The manager might cede some part of their role to machines, especially in areas where data is abundant and speed is of the essence. But the manager will also develop new skills in other areas and become more effective in what they do.

The fear that machines will steal jobs has existed since the time of the cotton gin in 1793. Every new technology brings in the same fear. The introduction of the typewriter in the early 1900s put the clerks who wrote documents by hand out of a job. Around seventy years later, the introduction of the computer eliminated typists. While technology eliminated some jobs, it made others at work more productive and enhanced their human potential. The deployment of intelligent machines in the workplace will transform jobs at every level into more complex ones, necessitating humans upskilling to meet the new demands.

As an example of how this could play out, let's look at the impact of automation on the banking industry in India over the last thirty years.

In 1980, Indian banks were dreary places where customers needed to deal with multiple bank officials who sat across glass barriers with grills. There were multiple counters for various transactions, and each counter had long queues. The bank officers would manage huge books and make multiple entries, and their supervisors would then do the same. Whether you were withdrawing a small sum of money or updating your account information, you would get the feeling that the bank was the master and was doing you a favour by allowing you access to your own money. The bank employees working behind the counters were an unhappy lot, as their job involved doing the same tasks and dealing with frustrated customers.

Banks faced pressure from increasing costs and competition from private banks. They looked at automation as a solution to both inefficiency and a better customer experience. However, the launch of the first steps towards bank automation sparked an uproar and loud protests among bank employees.[6] In a job-scarce country, employment with a bank ranked very highly among white-collar jobs, and it looked like these jobs would go away with the introduction of computers. One could scarcely imagine then how automation in the banking industry significantly changed the customer experience, increased operational efficiencies, created multiple new jobs and completely repositioned the role of bank employee.

Today, most people probably visit their bank branch once a year or even less frequently, as technology has enabled us to perform most banking tasks online. The bank looks a bit different now, and any remnants of the mesh cages seem to have disappeared. The ones that have not changed are few, mostly in small places where the reach of the internet is limited. Today's bank is a sleek office that has discussion areas where you meet up with a smart bank officer who can advise you on your investment needs. The officer has at her fingertips all your bank-related information. In fact, in many instances, the same discussion can happen at home or over a video link. And what happened to passbooks that used to be updated and rubber-stamped? Never mind!

In 1991, India had about 60,000 bank branches. In the three decades since then, this number has grown to about 160,000, with much of this growth spread out across the country.[7] In 1991, there was a deposit portfolio of Rs 2.38 trillion and a credit portfolio of Rs 1.32 trillion; by March 2021, the deposit portfolio had crossed Rs 151 trillion and the credit portfolio had come close to Rs 110 trillion. The industry offers close to 1.5 million direct jobs and 4 million indirect jobs.

Interestingly, the number of jobs in the bank at the middle level has risen more than at the lower level. Today, the bank employee has a much higher order of skills than their peers in the past. In addition to counting and disbursing currency, they are now advising customers on the best option for their investment or on how to better structure a housing loan. The customer no longer dreads going to the bank and sees the banker as a trusted advisor. On a personal note, I've still retained my passbook as a souvenir.

All Jobs Need You to Upskill

Sometime in 2019, the Organisation for Economic Co-operation and Development (OECD) predicted that by 2035, new automation technologies were likely to eliminate 14 per cent of the world's jobs and radically transform another 32 per cent of jobs. We can already see that happening about ten years before the predicted date, as advances in technology are accelerating the shift. Technology available today can handle not only jobs that are repetitive and manual but also bring in significant automation in jobs that are considered highly skilled as well as others. We saw this in the example of the airline pilot, the call centre worker and surgeon. In areas dominated by knowledge workers like researchers, coders, law clerks, writers, etc., jobs are being disrupted faster.

For a while, jobs have been the dominant component of work. A lot of time is spent defining the level of a particular job based on how work is done, the years of experience and skills needed, how it is supervised and so on. There are a variety of job evaluation methods and frameworks that focus on this effort. Every HR practice area, from hiring to compensation to career and performance, is linked to the definition of a particular job in the company's framework. However, this process is static and doesn't consider how quickly jobs can change. It's time to now rethink jobs in terms of skills needed and whether a particular job needs to be done by a human, machine or both and then map the job in terms of position and rate of change. Skills can be acquired and improved as jobs evolve and change. Hence, we need to spend more time on skills than on jobs.

Unfortunately, most skills have a limited life span and require constant updating. In the past, a surgeon could expect the skills she acquired during training and medical school to largely remain relevant during her practice years. A good surgeon would, of course, keep themselves updated with new methods, instruments and drugs periodically, but it was an incremental learning approach. Today, skills don't last that long because of advancements in technology and knowledge. A surgeon would need to reskill every decade or so. The same holds true for every profession.

You might be familiar with the concept of the half-life of radioactive elements. In simple terms, it's the interval of time required for one-half of the atomic nuclei of a radioactive sample to decay. The same concept can be applied to skills. The half-life of a skill is the time it takes for a particular skill to become irrelevant in search advertisements. In many areas, the half-life of skills is considered five years and in some, even three years. It means that if you don't stay updated, you will struggle to stay relevant.

In organizations of the future, the focus will be on the problem to be solved or value to be created rather than on the job. Organizations will view people as individuals possessing skills and capabilities that they can dynamically utilize to complete specific tasks in accordance with business priorities. Once the activity is over, the individual will find or be assigned new activities to remain employed, as long as their skills are relevant. By basing human-resource decisions on skills more than jobs, organizations can still have a scalable, manageable and more equitable way of operating.

Coming back to the question of the competition with the robot, as humans, we need to compete based on our skills and not assume that a job will always be on hand. Further, we need to look at our individual ability to add value beyond what can be done by automated systems and intelligent machines, learn to operate in a digital environment, improve our human skills and continually adapt to new ways of working and new occupations.

In a labour market that is more automated, digital and dynamic, each one of us will benefit from having a set of skills that can be improved. We can broadly bucket our skills into three categories. Regardless of the industry one works in, a combination of these three categories, each with varying levels of proficiency, will consistently be required.

a. Skills that focus on the human at work or human skills, where we can add value beyond what can be done by automated systems at intelligent machines. This would include skills like critical thinking, human intelligence, communication, ethical judgement and so on.
b. Skills that are technical for the role or technical skills. These would change with the role, but examples include coding, accounting, data analysis, designing, etc.
c. Skills that are related to the industry or domain. These would include industry knowledge, process knowledge, competitive structure, pricing, etc.

If we take the example of a bank employee looking at the future, in terms of human skills, what we would focus on are empathy and listening, communication, problem finding and solving, trust and reliability.

In terms of technical skills, the bank employee would need to be competent in handling the software deployed at the bank, able to work with tools to analyse the data and draw inferences, to work with data and present it in a useful way, etc. The employee would also need to be conversant in basic problem solving on technical matters like loan structuring, investing, etc.

And in terms of domain, the employee needs to be conversant with the changing regulations on banking and taxation, have knowledge of financial markets and economics, have knowledge of the various products sold by the bank, etc., so that they can guide their customers correctly.

A Passport for Skills?

Over time, workers have depended on formal educational degrees and certificates of employment to land jobs. The future of work doesn't necessarily employ you based on your qualifications and experience. Take, for example, a plumber who has a set of tools and a pair of hands without any documented proof of his skills, qualifications or work experience. Even though he might be highly qualified or even formally trained, there is no way a new employer can gauge the skills he possesses without putting him through an evaluation process. This can be solved in the future with the creation of a 'skill passport'.

Just as you need a passport to enter a new country, in the future, a job seeker can present a passport of the skills they have acquired for entry into a new organization. Your country of citizenship issues a passport that holds basic information about you, records your visits to various countries and details the duration of your stay in those countries. Similarly, a skill passport will have a record of your base qualifications certified by your university, the jobs you held, the skills and expertise you acquired and additional endorsements based on what you accomplished post-qualification.

A skill passport could be an electronic document that will standardize information about your skills and proficiency. Potential employers could just upload this information into their hiring process, saving the effort of verifying and assessing your skills. Once databases are more uniformly accessible, the hiring system could even assess your suitability for a role with minimal work left for the hiring manager. While this may not work for specialized jobs needing people in small numbers, any bulk hiring, especially in the informal sectors needing skilled labour, will migrate to using digital skill passports in the future.

A skill passport will allow companies to make hiring decisions based on the strength and relevance of an individual's skills and not on their career histories or professional networks. This document will work across countries and companies. Using a skill passport will make employment decisions non-biased and help companies recruit from a diverse talent pool. The skills passport is envisioned as a digital document based on blockchain technology that is secure. The document will list the skills the passport holder possesses and provide validation information, either from the employer or an independent certifying agency. The skill passport will be updated with new skills or changes in competency levels as the holder's career progresses.

The skills passport will instantly map the applicant to open positions that the information in the passport will match from the employer's point of view. A skill passport could also serve as a gating document, reflecting an individual's skill level in the context of various jobs. The certification could either be at a company level or an industry level. There is also the possibility that employers will validate the self-certification of skills over the course of employment as the concept matures. When an individual leaves the organization, the passport will provide them with an updated document.

Initial skill passports would need to be issued at the country level and connected to citizen identification. Considering that in the future, many countries in the world will be experiencing labour shortages, having a skill passport will also aid in the migration of skilled individuals to places that need their skills. Access to the skill recognition process is a constant struggle for migrant workers, and migrants frequently end up with jobs that are at a lower qualification level and end up wasting their skills. For example, a doctor entering a new country often needs to redo her medical certification. A skill passport will save them from that effort, and as the concept of skilling evolves, it's likely that the information contained in their skill passport will allow them to start with their job without going through re-certification and a prolonged wait.

Conclusion

Changing our world view from jobs to skills gives us a different way of approaching the new world of work. We can view this as an evolution of the human at work, and the move from jobs to skills will yield significant benefits to both organizations and employees. In most places, skills are changing much faster than jobs ever could, and an employee wanting to benefit from this change will need to reskill quickly in the direction of change.

To adapt to the rapidly accelerating pace of technological change, each one of us will have to develop ways to learn and keep our skills current in a systematic, rigorous, experimental and long-term way. The worry about robots taking away our jobs won't go away entirely, as none of us can predict accurately what will happen to our present job in the future. But by changing our focus from the job to skills, we will always have new areas for us to work on. At a time when speed, agility, and innovation rule the day, people expect more meaning, choice, growth and autonomy at work. The robot is a friend who can help us with this objective by taking on some of our uninteresting work, allowing us to ideate and find new work to do.

Exercise

For the profession you are in, list down the skills in each of the three categories.

a. Skills that focus on the human at work or human skills.
b. Skills that are technical for the role or technical skills.
c. Skills that are related to the industry or domain skills.

A simple way to start is to take the job description your company has for your current role and the next two immediate roles to which you could get promoted. Another way to start is to look at job advertisements for roles you are interested in. You will now have a list of skills that are relevant for you. It's perfectly all right if the list is long and some part of it is aspirational.

Once you have identified the skills that your profession needs for the future, it's time to assess your proficiency against these skills. For simplicity, you can term these proficiency levels as beginner, competent and expert. At different points in time, each of us will be at different levels in each of our skills. Do an honest assessment of your level, as this exercise is for your benefit alone.

The next step is to identify the skills needed for the same job in ten years. If ten years is too long, then do five years. You might need to speak to an expert in the field to get an idea. This section is futuristic and does not need to be accurate. Holding all variables constant, future employment is more strongly associated with proficiency in future skills and so are higher incomes.

Here's an illustrative example:

Profession: **Software engineer** (banking & financial services)

	Skill	**Proficiency**
Human Skills	Communication (written) Teamwork Giving feedback Business presentations	Competent Competent Beginner Beginner
Technical Skills	Coding: C++, Java, Python Software testing / debugging Object oriented design	Competent Expert Beginner
Domain Skills	Banking Capital markets Insurance	Beginner Competent Competent

Future Skills (Five-Year Horizon)

User requirement analysis; consulting skills; cross-cultural adaptation; conflict resolution; negotiation.

Cloud services—infrastructure as a service (IaaS), software as a service (SaaS), Amazon Web Services (AWS); data and analytics—databases, data structures, algorithms and frameworks; AI tools and frameworks; cybersecurity literacy; computational and algorithmic thinking.

Banking regulations—EU Payment Services Directive 3 (PSD3) and Payment Services Regulations (PSR), basic accounting.

Training Plan

i. Consulting skills training programme—external (IIM)
ii. Cross-cultural skills programme—internal.

Certification Plan

iii. EU banking regulation certification
iv. AWS certification
v. Basic accounting

Once you have a sheet like the one above, speak openly about your need for upskilling with your manager. Often, people don't speak about their development needs out of fear that they might be perceived negatively as someone lacking job competence. If you discuss your plan and reasons, it's likely that you will be presented with opportunities to develop skills while in your current job. Be honest and clear on why you would want to upskill as well as the fact that you will continue to be relevant to the company. Many companies offer certifications that prove that you have a baseline understanding of the skill as well as indicate your level of competence. Certifications also provide a formal endorsement, which is particularly useful if you are transitioning careers and do not have enough experience to showcase. For example, those transitioning to an HR career have particularly found GPHR and SPHR certifications quite useful. You will be surprised at the variety of options that are available, provided you have a plan for what you want.

Secondly, plan your time. Upskilling programmes often require a major investment of your time, and if the programme is not of immediate use, it's quite likely that you will have to do it on your own time. For example, if a company offers a graduate degree programme, you should be prepared to give up some weekends towards finishing. Or if you are signing up for a stretch assignment or a job rotation to acquire certain skills, be aware of how to manage your time in order to complete the programme.

Thirdly, remember that upskilling is not only about designed programmes delivered to you or choosing from a menu. Be prepared to use online resources, as well as the opportunity for hands-on skill development by working part-time or on gig projects. In some cases, it might be a faster way to acquire skills.

Whether your objective is to remain relevant in your current role or to prepare for a future role, don't forget that upskilling is something each one of us needs to do all the time. Jobs and the skills needed for those jobs are changing constantly, and you are expected to keep pace with the skills needed as jobs evolve. Don't get left behind in the skills game.

Chapter 2

Painting a Masterpiece While Clearing Your Mail

Many people feel they must multitask because everybody else is multitasking, but this is partly because they are all interrupting each other so much.

—Marilyn vos Savant

Michelangelo is widely regarded as one of the greatest artists of all time. His works are expansive and span painting, sculpture, drawing, architecture and poetry. Michelangelo primarily thought of himself as a sculptor, though practice with multiple art forms was not uncommon among artists of his time. Michelangelo was in his early twenties when he was commissioned to create a statue representing the biblical hero, David. He was offered a colossal block of marble, which had been previously provided to two other artists. Both artists had abandoned their work after finding the assignment too challenging.

Despite discouragement from his friends, Michelangelo took up the monumental challenge of carving the figure. He was twenty-five years old when he started working on 'David'. He first created a wax model and submerged it in water. He then slowly lowered the water level as he worked on the piece of marble over the next two years. He worked outdoors in an open courtyard, exposing himself to the elements. He worked from dawn to dusk and was exhausted at night, covered with marble chips and dust. Nothing distracted him from releasing 'David', who was housed within the marble. In 1504, Michelangelo finished sculpting 'David'. Between 1508 and 1512, Michelangelo painted the ceiling of the Sistine Chapel in Rome. These two works are considered among the greatest works of art that define human civilization.

Although Michelangelo was known for taking up more work than he could deliver and was terrible at delivering as per commitments, you could not doubt his focus and almost superhuman capacity for hard work. He wouldn't allow any distraction to take him away from his projects, sparing little time for anything other than preparing, drawing and then painting or sculpting. He pursued his projects with such vigour that, while on the job, he lived a very frugal life. A little bread and wine were all he needed for supper. He would often rise in the middle of the night to resume his work by candlelight. On some occasions, he would be too tired to undress and would sleep in his work clothes, ready to start again as soon as he was refreshed by a little sleep. During the time he was painting the Sistine Chapel, he was so focused on completing the work to perfection that he refused to meet anyone, even at his own house, to not lose focus.

Given that Michelangelo lived in a time when there were no digital devices to interrupt his work with notification pings, he could have shut himself in his workspace and sculpted for a couple of years if he wanted. However, there were distractions all around. He lived in a time of intense political tension between his hometown of Florence and Rome. He also had a wide variety of interests across the arts. There was also social pressure for artists to be part of their patron's court. However, Michelangelo ignored everything to focus, producing not only 'David' and 'The Last Judgement' but many more masterpieces of genius.

Most of us are not tasked with producing works of art, but there is no reason why we cannot produce works of enduring value. If you were to list down ten things that you produced in the last month, be it a presentation, a proposal, a piece of code or something else, which of these would you be proud of? Also, would the quality of your output change dramatically if you had been allowed to work undistracted?

Today, it's rare to get the time and space to focus on work without distraction. Studies on workplace productivity suggest that most office workers do less than an hour of focused work each day.[1] You can try testing this yourself using the timer on your phone. Start with a significant task that you need to finish. It could be a presentation, a proposal or something similar. Start the timer when you begin the task and stop it the minute any distraction crops up. Distractions include anything that makes you shift your focus from the task. A pop-up notification, a co-worker stopping by to chat, a call or message on your phone or simply losing focus. You can repeat this experiment on different days of the week.

If your start-to-stop time is above fifteen minutes, then you are in the upper quartile of productive workers. The idea is to move this time to as close to an hour as possible using simple techniques and to then get multiple such productive hours in a working day. This will improve your efficiency, reduce stress, allow you to produce superior output and, more importantly, let you leave the office earlier.

This is what I gathered when I documented my typical workday. The first thing I did when I woke up in the morning was look at my phone. Usually, there are some WhatsApp notifications that demand attention. Then I scrolled through my mail to see what I missed when I was asleep. This is more out of habit, and it usually only serves to distract my attention. Once I reached the office, I was drawn into a couple of meetings that I had not planned for. After these meetings, I spent some time attending to emails until it was time for lunch with a colleague. Post-lunch, I convinced myself that I would focus on important tasks that included a presentation to the board. Halfway through finishing the presentation, I received a call to respond to a news query regarding an apparent crisis. By the time I finished attending to it, my ability to focus had largely left me, and I spent the remaining time attending to some irrelevant tasks before leaving for the day. The day felt very busy, but in reality, I hadn't done much. During the commute home, I promised myself that tomorrow I would focus better.

You would be familiar with this kind of day at work. The fact is that such days are common and make us feel tired but unfulfilled. Let's now look at what we can do to get the most productivity out of our days at work. We may not be sculpting David, but we would love to produce work that is enduring, appreciated and makes us feel good. Also, it will be great if we can enable our colleagues to limit distractions and find focus. So, let's explore how to make ourselves more productive and create a work environment that enables us to reduce low-priority work and commit our time to what is important.

There are two reasons that prevent us from achieving focus at work. The first is about not having a clear idea of what we want to accomplish. The second is to do with what is termed work creep, where non-priorities enter our workday.

What You Want to Accomplish

In Lewis Carroll's classic children's tale, *Alice in Wonderland*, there is a conversation between Alice and the Cheshire Cat. Alice asks the Cat, 'Would you tell me, please, which way I ought to go from here?' 'That depends a good deal on where you want to get to,' says the Cat. 'I don't much care where,' says Alice. 'Then it doesn't matter which way you go,' says the Cat. 'So long as I get SOMEWHERE,' Alice adds as an explanation. 'Oh, you're sure to do that', says the Cat, 'if you only walk long enough.'

When you are clear on the purpose and the time by which you want to accomplish something, focusing and avoiding distractions become much easier. You could be motivated by needing to submit work of high quality for a business meeting or you might have a career goal in mind, such as being selected to attend a leadership programme. Start by listing down what you would like to keep your focus on. It will be a basket, with some work needing to be delivered in a short span of time and others over a longer duration. Then all you need to do during your focus time is take out projects from this basket and work on them without allowing any distractions. Visualizing your goals in this fashion helps remind your brain that this is focus time.

Setting goals provides you with a sense of direction and motivation. This helps you focus. One of the methods for setting good goals is using what is labelled as the SMART technique. SMART is an acronym for Specific, Measurable, Achievable, Realistic, and Timely.

- The goals you have should be well defined, clear and unambiguous. (Specific)
- You should be able to measure your progress towards your goals using a set of clear criteria. (Measurable)
- The goals should be those that are possible to achieve. Having a goal that is too ambitious is a sure way to lose focus. (Achievable)
- The goals should be within reach, realistic and meet your overall purpose for your career or life. (Realistic)
- And finally, you should have an idea of the start and end dates so that you can take up work and finish at the right time. (Timely)

While picking tasks from your goal basket, you should not take out more than one item at a time. If you want to take up something else, then you need to put the item you are working on back in the basket. You can do this after you have spent the allotted focus time for that task. Under no circumstances should you work on more than one item from the basket at a time.

Dealing with Distractions without Losing Focus

In today's workplace, more than half of a knowledge worker's time is spent on activities that can be performed even while being distracted. This work involves coordination, follow-ups, meetings or other activities that do not require a large amount of focus. Once you gain some experience, this work becomes routine. Most of us can also simultaneously work on multiple things. For example, clearing our email inboxes while attending a meeting. There is nothing wrong with doing this, as this component of our work is not going to go away. These are non-cognitive-demanding logistical activities that can be performed well even when distracted. However, these activities do not create enduring value.

The idea is to bring focus while doing the remaining work; usually, the part that is complex demands focus and often gets postponed. This part of work pushes us to deliver our best and needs our complete attention. If we can manage to give this part of our work our undivided focus, we will be able to produce better results and be more competent and productive.

Cal Newport, an American professor at Georgetown University in Washington DC, pioneered the concept of 'Deep Work', which he defines as 'professional activities performed in a state of distraction-free concentration that push your cognitive capabilities to the limit. These efforts create new value, improve your skills and are hard to replicate.'[2]

What Michelangelo did was deep work. While painting 'The Creation of Adam' on the ceiling of the Sistine Chapel, Michelangelo painted alone, lying on a high scaffolding on his back and looking upward for the full day. This was a feat of supreme physical endurance and intellectual and artistic mastery. His attention to every detail and his overall execution exemplify the power of genius. By then, Michelangelo was a busy man, his time being pulled by many demands from other clients. Yet while painting the ceiling of the chapel, he was able to devote large chunks of time to one pursuit alone. While he could devote the full day, Prof. Newport's research shows us that the time a modern office worker needs to devote to deep work is about three hours at a time. For those three hours, we need to be away from anything that distracts us from our pursuit. This includes modern tools, such as instant messengers, emails, social media, infotainment sites and so on. These let in distractions that fragment our attention and chip away at the core of the three hours. To begin, aim to dedicate three hours of deep work per week. As you progress, your aim should be to increase it to three hours per workday. Once you have achieved that level of focus, you will be in the top percentile of your profession in terms of productivity and on your way to deliver superior results consistently.

Before we move ahead, let's try out the idea. This practice session is for just one week, Monday to Friday, during office hours. There are just two simple exercises for you to do.

First exercise: If you are used to having your phone next to you when you work, then keep it away and clearly mark the deep work time. The duration of time is up to you, but it should not be less than an hour to start with. Set an alarm if you want, based on your estimate, to complete the task at hand. You cannot go to your phone until the buzzer rings.

Second exercise: When you go to some meetings, you will not check your phone for the duration of the meeting. Leave it behind if you want. You can decide the meetings for which you want to try this out.

Score yourself during both exercises—one point for every success and minus two points for every failure. See what comes up; there is no right or wrong. If you manage a positive score at the end of the week, you are on your way. If the score is negative, try the same exercise again the following week. You will get there if you stay on course.

You can try some other practices, such as closing extra tabs on your computer or turning off your social media notifications while at work. You may also have some other distractions that are specific to your job, and you can choose them for the above exercise. The idea is to avoid distractions and gradually increase the duration for which you can focus.

Now, let's explore some techniques to avoid workplace distractions.

Fixing your work style preferences: Each of us has our own work style preferences, so based on what you prefer, dedicate a set number of hours a day for deep work. The ideal time chunk is three hours, but some keep two hours and others keep four. It does not matter, so long as the duration suits you. The key is to be consistent so that your brain recognizes this as a pattern. The other approach is to fix days of the week for deep work. For example, having no-meeting days in the week or not being available for calls and casual discussions on some days. With remote working being acceptable, you will find this easier to schedule on your non-office days. Slotting in deep work hours can become easier once you get better at it. Then, you will be able to switch to your deep work mode seamlessly.

Create work rituals for yourself: I was once meeting a well-known senior corporate executive. When I met him at his home office, I was surprised to see such a sparse desk. All that he had on the table was a notepad and a pen. I have met many executives over the years, but I have rarely seen such a clear demonstration of a non-distracting environment for a discussion. A clean desk was a signal, both to the host as well as to me, that we needed to concentrate and focus on the one single task at hand. Other work rituals you might want to consider are the location you choose to occupy during focus time, instructions to your team regarding work disturbances, background music, noise-cancelling headphones, etc. Having a work ritual tells your mind that this is the time for deep work without distractions.

Prioritize ruthlessly: We all face multiple demands and struggle with saying no to various requests for our time. Your boss might assign urgent tasks, a co-worker might invite you for a coffee or someone might drop in at your desk to chat. If you want to accomplish something meaningful in your planned deep work time, then prioritization is important. If you have other important tasks that need to be finished, then you need to draw a list of priorities and schedule time and the order in which they will be taken up.

Tracking time spent: One of the difficulties faced in doing focused work is that we do not always have a track of how our day goes. As you get more accustomed to doing focused work, the next stage is to increase the time that is available by tracking usage. Time is a finite resource that you need to be stingy about. You could either use an online productivity tool or a pen and paper to find out how you spend your time on a daily or weekly basis. You simply need to put down the main activities and the time you spend on each and look at them on a weekly basis. This will show you how to steal away extra time and get more done.

Be stingy about meetings: Someone once joked that if you had to explain, in one word, why the human race has not achieved its full potential, it would be 'meetings'. Yet meetings are a part of modern office life, and we need to find a way around them.[3] One strategy is to divide meetings into three categories. The first one is where decisions are made, and you have a stake in those decisions. The second category are meetings that are for sharing information, where someone makes a presentation to a larger group. The third category is what can be termed 'nose-counting' meetings that you need to attend so that you are visible and seen by your managers or leaders. The first category is a must-do, where you should go with prepared points and note follow-up actions. The second category is largely avoidable, and you can see if the information can be shared without attending the meeting. The third category is tricky, but with some planning, you can ensure you are seen and counted at the right meeting. By dividing meetings, you will find that you will have a whole lot of time for focused work.

Blinkers help horses: Distractions, especially the ones that involve a phone screen, are something that takes away our focus. In fact, research[4] shows that it takes an average of twenty-three minutes to regain focus after a distraction. If you are someone who works while having email and messenger notifications active, you will feel the pressure to drop what you are doing to attend to the urgent and the unimportant. There is a reason why horses wear blinkers, and we can use this idea for ourselves. You should simply not have any channels like notifications, sound, etc. that can catch your attention while doing deep work.

Conference calls: In the early days of the pandemic, as we were all isolated in our homes, we found that conference calls were a great way to keep in touch with colleagues and to show our bosses that we were working and contributing. Like any other office tool, these calls became overused, with each of us making multiple such calls every week. If you add all your calls for the week, you will be surprised by the time you are spending looking at other people on a small screen without clear purpose.

Planning your time: Dedicate about fifteen minutes at the end of your workday to building your schedule for the following day. During this planning process, make note of your task list, including what is part of your short-term and long-term goals. Having a plan gives a boost to your productivity, and soon you could have a forty-hour week instead of a sixty-hour one.

The ability to focus on the important gives you an edge in today's workplace. It also brings satisfaction and meaning into our lives because we feel that we have accomplished something important at the end of the day or week. You will find the quality of your output is proportional to the time spent and the amount of focus put into your work.

Imagine two college students working on an essay that is due for submission on Monday. One of them starts working on Sunday evening and the other decides to work on the essay a few days earlier. The first student has less time and the second one has more time. By logic, the quality of the work produced by the second student should be better as he has more time, but this is only partly true. The first student, putting in three hours of focused effort, will be able to produce better work than the second student working on the essay longer but with distractions. In order to produce something exceptional, we should try to combine the planning of the second student with the focus of the first student. That's what paining a masterpiece is all about.

The Story of a Detox Before Digital

A digital detox involves voluntarily halting the use of any digital device for a specific period of time. However, the idea of unplugging and living a simple life is not new. Henry David Thoreau was an American writer. Sometime in the mid-1800s, he went to live for two years in a log cabin he built with his own hands near Walden Pond in Massachusetts. He detailed his reflections in the book *Walden: Life in the Woods*, which was first published in

1854. The book is an illustration of living among natural surroundings and the learnings from his experiment with simple living are relevant even today.

Thoreau tells us about how he built his cabin in the spring of 1845 using his own hands. He borrows or scrounges most of the building materials from friends. Thoreau also starts a small garden, where he grows a modest quantity of vegetables for his sustenance. While at the cabin, he spends most of his mornings working in his garden or house. He spends his afternoons and evenings in contemplation, reading and taking long walks in the surrounding countryside. His experiences reinforce the values of austerity, simplicity and solitude.

Thoreau consistently emphasizes the minimalism of his lifestyle and the contentment that one can derive from it. He repeatedly contrasts his own freedom with the imprisonment of others who devote their lives to accumulating material things. In his words describing his experiment, 'I went to the woods because I wished to live deliberately, to front only the essential facts of life, and see if I could not learn what it had to teach, and not, when I came to die, discover that I had not lived.' He adds, 'I wanted to live deep and suck out all the marrow of life, to live so sturdily and Spartan-like.'[5]

We can't all go and construct a cabin by the pond as Thoreau did. In the first place, our friends won't lend us their land, and constructing log cabins on your own is difficult. But most of all, we wouldn't be able to live without our digital devices for a day. Come to think of it, a digital detox might be one of the most difficult things we ever take up.

A detox is what you do to remove toxins from your body. These toxins can negatively affect health. A detox is usually done through dietary changes and other interventions in a controlled manner. Similarly, a digital detox helps us take a break from digital devices and social media feeds. This has proven to have a lot of benefits and has improved people's health.

I'm not advocating a full detox along the lines of living by Walden Pond. Most of us don't need a full separation; we just need to balance our use of digital devices for productivity. Here are a few simple ways to achieve a detox while retaining the use of digital devices.

To start, you can take a survey on an online tool[6] to check the level of your digital addiction. There are many such surveys available online. These online tests will make you answer a few questions and show how attached you are to your devices. It's important to be aware of where you are before you take the first steps towards detox. Once you know the extent of your dependency, you can follow the steps below.

If you're working full-time on your computer, plan breaks that force you to go away from any digital device. For example, your break from the computer should not involve you using your phone. Stand up, move and do something that doesn't require staring at screens. You could go for a short walk, do a quick workout, wash your mug, make a cup of tea, look out the window, read a book, etc. These breaks will energize you for when you're back at the computer. You also give your eyes time to rest, which will take away the feeling of tiredness at the end of your workday. Connecting with nature is another great way to get away from your screen. If you are lucky enough to work in an office that provides green spaces or even has windows that allow you to look far, build this into your work routine.

The next step is to make a list of all the apps that are active on your phone and desktop. Remove all those that are not essential for your work or connections. Be judicious with the use of apps that feed you information or serve as entertainment; either delete the ones that distract you or move them to a folder that is not directly accessible. More importantly, disable all notifications, as they have a huge impact on your ability to focus. You can designate a particular time of the day to check for messages and respond to those that require attention. Rarely does a notification warrant an urgent response, interrupting our work or train of thought.

The third step is to examine your digital routine from start to finish. One of the best things you can do is not check your phone when you wake up and go to bed. When you wake up, our brain needs some time to warm up for the day. Experts say it's usually about thirty minutes to an hour, and if you give it immediate work to do, it's likely that it will leave you fatigued for the rest of the day. The first part of your day is for yourself—to connect with nature, family or yourself. The same happens before going to bed. Your brain needs time away from screens, as blue light inhibits the release of melatonin, a chemical essential for sleep. Our ancestors used to sleep once the sun set, and we are not too far away in terms of our evolution to have adjusted to artificial light. So, controlling light exposure towards bedtime is a good way to get peaceful sleep.

The last part of doing a partial digital detox is to avoid using a digital device as a solution to boredom. Most of us do this without even realizing what we are up to—we use our devices when we are in a meeting, in the lift or even when we are with friends. If you need to go to your device when you are involved in something, it's a signal to you that you are not fully into whatever activity you are doing. You either need to return to what you were doing before being distracted or find something more interesting to do.

Once you have started following the above three simple rules, you can attempt a full detox for half a day or even a full day on the weekend. You can decide what time and day of the week to do this. You will find this refreshing and uplifting. The fear of missing out, the feeling of urgency, etc. are just unconscious perceptions that we built over the years, and a digital detox can help eliminate some of these compulsions with a little training and determination.

Once you have mastered the ability to switch off from your device as needed, you can rebuild your digital usage in a way that works best for your needs. Some people do this by following a small number of social media accounts, while others have a no-device day. Create your own rule and make it work, so that you can take pride in what you have accomplished with your own version of the Walden Pond.

Getting Others to Join Deep Work

While we have focused on individual productivity, it's also useful to get your team involved in the concept of deep work. Doing so will improve team productivity while also allowing you to do more. Whether you work remotely or not, you can follow some simple rules to enhance team productivity.

The first rule is to discourage people from always being available. Having a regular shutdown time reduces stress levels and allows people to unwind at the end of the workday. The team should have a rule that contacting colleagues after the defined team shutdown time should be rare and only in case of an emergency.

The second rule is to reduce meetings. Make it clear to the team that meetings will be held to accomplish a purpose, will have a clear agenda and only those needed will be invited. Some teams have developed the practice of front-loading all meetings to Mondays or Tuesdays so that the rest of the week is available for deep work. Another great idea is to have designated 'no-meeting' days during the week.

The third rule is to establish team norms to avoid distractions. These could be simple ones such as an email does not need an instant reply, team members should respect each other's time depending on their status updates as available or do not disturb and casual interactions can happen only during certain times of the day. Make these team norms clear to everyone who joins the team, so that it becomes a part of work life.

The final rule is a little difficult to follow for managers. This rule is to minimize distractions caused by your actions. These could include sending them meaningless tasks and ideas, calling for unplanned meetings and so on. As far as possible, reduce communication channels and information flow. Most teams have too many channels, which adds to the clutter. Have a single channel to communicate task lists and completion schedules.

As a manager, you should lead a culture of focus. You can have a periodic review of the project inventory and to-do list with the team. If the team does not list their commitments in an organized fashion with set timelines, prioritization and completion become difficult. It's a good practice to share team priorities and make them visible to everyone. The early quality gurus[7] insisted on the list being displayed on a board near the workplace. There was a reason behind this—you couldn't miss it, and it worked.[8]

Allow people to prioritize and say no to tasks that don't fit into the goals. You need to create a feeling of psychological safety for your team and support them when they adhere to planned schedules. They should even feel comfortable enough to say no to demands you bring in if they don't fit into the agreed-upon list.

Deep Work Beyond Office

We can compartmentalize our lives into certain distinct areas, such as family, health, career and so on. Each of these areas can benefit from our ability to focus. While we looked at work in the earlier section, the same principles can be applied to family interactions, health goals or our hobbies. Work does occupy a larger portion of our lives, but we have other important parts of our lives where focus can improve the quality of what we do. How many of us are guilty of being drawn away from a family dinner to attend office calls or end up being distracted with work matters while engaging with children?

These focus techniques can be tweaked for a non-work context and easily adopted at home. For example, set a no-phone rule at designated times during the day or a no-email day during the weekend. One of the rules I have been able to consistently apply over time is the no-email rule. One day of the weekend, either Saturday or Sunday, I do not touch my office laptop. Apart from the physical and mental break, it also helps me rejuvenate for the week ahead.

In addition to work, set goals for your life outside of work. It could be learning to play a musical instrument, spending time with your kids or engaging in a home renovation project. Just pick one goal for a period of time. For example, if you pick health, then your goal could be to lose four kilos over the next four months. It does not mean that you must neglect other commitments, but you must attend to them during your non-focus time.

* * *

Most of us have lost our ability to go deep into what we do. Whether we are office workers working on tasks or creative ones trying to do something beautiful, we seem to spend our days in a frantic blur of meetings, emails, conference calls and social media without realizing that time is passing us by at a rapid pace. Using some of the above techniques can help you create a culture of focus for yourself and your team. By doing this, you can focus on work that really matters and create everyday masterpieces that will bear your name.

Chapter 3

Dr Jekyll and Mr Manager

I'm a leader, not a follower. Unless it's a dark place; then you are going first.

—Unknown

Robert Louis Stevenson's interesting novella *The Strange Case of Dr Jekyll and Mr Hyde* set in nineteenth-century London, is about Dr Jekyll, a kind and respected doctor much loved by his patients. However, the good doctor has an evil side to him that is not always easy to repress. He develops a serum that compartmentalizes his dark side. By doing this, he is able to transform into his alter ego as and when he wants. He names the beastly side of him Mr Hyde. While the doctor can initially control the transformation, over time, he loses this control when Mr Hyde appears and Dr Jekyll recedes to the background. During the years I have spent in the people practice, I have met managers and employees who fit into this story quite well without even needing a serum.

It's never easy working with someone whose style does not align with yours. During a recent interview, I questioned a candidate about his plans to leave a company that met all the criteria for being a great place to work. His response was honest, and he mentioned a manager from hell with horns, hooves and a pointy tail. Unfortunately, he is not the first or last employee to leave a company because of a manager. Toxic workplaces and managers who contribute to creating bad work environments are more common than we think and lead to mental health issues, low productivity and early exits.[1]

Many years ago, a member of my sales team narrated a compelling story. His job involved selling large turnkey projects to automobile companies. After a difficult sales pursuit lasting many months, he managed to land an order of significant size from a well-known company. What was even more impressive was that the sale came at a very marginal discount. Considering that many of the large sales in this business came at large discounts, this was clearly a very favourable deal. He excitedly called his manager to convey the good news and expected to be congratulated by him. His manager told him bluntly that the minor discount was unacceptable and asked him to go back and renegotiate the terms of the sale. That night, this salesperson suffered a mild heart attack, for which he was hospitalized and later underwent a long period of convalescence. On his return to work, he found that his manager had taken over the client relationship in his absence and renegotiated the deal. The manager had signed the deal by giving a much higher discount than the salesperson had initially offered, and seemed quite pleased with the outcome.

This story might seem odd and unbelievable, but I assure you, it's completely true. What's more surprising is that this manager had a fairly long career in the company and was quite brilliant on some dimensions. However, handling a team was not one of them. It's a matter of regret as to how much more could have been achieved if he could have handled people better and focused more on channelling his Dr Jekyll than his Mr Hyde.

The boss–subordinate relationship is never an easy one. Part of the difficulty comes from the power inequality in the relationship. Usually, when people gain authority over others, they tend to become more self-centred and less mindful of other people's needs. To compound the situation, not all team members behave equally with the boss and many complex aspects of human behaviour come into play. However, companies also have great managers whose teams flourish under them. In this chapter, we will attempt to distil the learnings from these good managers and filter out the practices from the bad ones.

Towards the latter part of the Covid-19 pandemic, we witnessed a huge exodus from the global workforce. This was creatively labelled as the 'great resignation of 2021'. In the US itself, over a six-month period, 24 million employees resigned from their jobs, leaving businesses scrambling to fill vacancies. Many studies have been conducted to understand why this happened. Despite the pandemic's uncertainty and signs of a possible slowdown, people were still willing to take a chance on changing their employer. The most common reasons employees quoted in their exit interview were connected to the work culture—toxicity in the workplace, bad managers and so on. We don't need to do research to illustrate this. A toxic workplace is ten times more likely to cause attrition than compensation.[2] As per a 2015 Gallup survey, half the employees who left their jobs did so because of a bad manager.[3]

While it is possible that a bad work culture has several origins, the single largest contributor usually originates from the way managers treat people. Managers who are toxic make others nervous and uncomfortable, impact morale, reduce productivity and, worst of all, encourage others to learn bad work practices. Just like one rotten apple in a barrel quickly spoils the rest of the fruit, bad managers influence others to become like them. In my experience, employees are more directly impacted by the culture in their immediate team, which is mostly controlled by how their manager behaves.

The composition of teams has changed due to automation and is likely to further change with the introduction of AI-based tools. This means that there are more supervisory and managerial positions than before. Today, in most large companies, one in five employees manages someone else. Unfortunately, companies do not spend as much on developing managers as they do on acquiring systems and tools.

Whether you are leading a small team or a larger unit, or heading the company itself, it's important to remind yourself that you are dealing with humans first and it's your job to do everything possible to make the workplace more human for those you lead. In this chapter, we will focus on distilling the serum or practices that make us more of Dr Jekyll and less of Mr Hyde.

Giving and Receiving Feedback

Imagine that you are playing a musical instrument on stage, but the organizers have forgotten to place a feedback amplifier. Without this small but essential device, the sound you hear as feedback will be the reflected sound from the auditorium. It will then be very difficult for you, as a musician, to know how well you are doing or to correct yourself. Similarly, as managers, we fail to provide enough direct feedback to our team members and expect them to perform based on reflected feedback from the larger environment they operate in.

All of us need feedback to perform well. As a manager, giving feedback is an important part of your job and it is best to have a uniform way of providing feedback to your team. While individuals may have different preferences for receiving feedback, I have found that a uniform and consistent managerial approach is best. Let's look at two methods of providing feedback that are helpful.

Declining Feedback or the 70:20:10 Method

Imagine that you and your team are making a simple mobile app for the return-to-work phase of a company's hybrid work model. The objective of the app is to enable people to schedule the days they will be in office and to block seats on those days in the transport system as well as in the office. Like any other project, this assignment can be broken into three phases: the basic concept wireframe, the main coding phase and the final finished stage. The Declining Feedback method, in simple terms, means that feedback to the team should be maximum in the first stage, moderate in the middle and least in the end. Let's see how to do this.

At the initial wireframe stage, the project is fully flexible to incorporate changes and the suggested changes can be easily incorporated with minimal effort. At the development stage, the project is half finished, but important changes can still be incorporated. At the final stage, most of the work is done, and any change requires time and effort that is disproportional to the impact of the change. The 70:20:10 rule represents the amount of feedback needed, and it can be accommodated at each stage of a project. The maximum feedback the team needs and can be safely given is at the first stage—that's 70 per cent of the feedback. The remaining 20 per cent is given at the body stage and the last 10 per cent, mainly relating to look and feel, choice of colours, fonts, etc., is reserved for the final stage. This method can be applied to anything—a presentation, an advertisement, a mailer, etc. The cardinal rule is not to be broken, i.e., you are not allowed to give 70 per cent of the feedback when only 10 per cent of the work remains to be done. A manager or supervisor should give maximum feedback when it is most useful and least disruptive to the team.

The other rule of the Declining Feedback method is about the type of feedback given. For example, if you are supervising the construction of a house, the early feedback would be about the structure, size of the rooms, positioning of the windows, the lintel height, etc. You would not be expected to give feedback about the colour, the living room or the kind of tiles that will be put in the bathroom. That kind of feedback should be reserved for Stage 3.

While this method of feedback sounds quite logical, in order for it to work, you also need to bring about a culture change in the workgroup. You must encourage people to show you their work and be open to feedback. In normal circumstances, most people are not willing to show raw output and hence miss the opportunity to gather useful feedback at the stage where it matters most. For example, how many of us will be willing to submit an essay that's raw and receive feedback at an early stage? Instead, we wait until the essay is reasonably done and then ask for input. The feedback that comes at a late stage requires considerable rework. As a rule, we don't like to show our incomplete work to peers or managers because of various fears. But for the Declining Feedback method to work, teams need to do exactly that. As a manager, you need to create a sense of safety, even for the juniors, so they can get feedback from you and the team. It's a fine balance between being regarded as a non-performer and someone who uses opportunities to get useful feedback. With enough practice, you will soon have a team that doesn't hesitate to showcase their work at different stages in an open manner.

At the initial stage, the feedback should focus on the overall plan and direction and chalk out the main concepts. There is no need to get into Stage 3 issues such as colours, logos and fonts. You should debate the project itself and focus on its goals, objectives and fundamental building blocks. It's also important that this part be recorded as part of the project documentation, as team members who come in later need to understand why certain decisions were taken at that time.

Then comes the middle stage. This is when the project slowly begins to resemble the final output in structure and form. At this stage, you want to confirm that the work is moving in the right direction and that no fundamental changes are needed. Again, it's important that your inputs are not seen as criticism and need to be synchronous with the feedback given in the earlier stage. This is the right stage to bring in other teams that might have a stake in the outcome, as there is still time to implement suggestions.

Then comes the last stage, where you have the final chance for feedback. This stage is before you move the app from the test server to the live stage. At this stage, you look at the colours, the logo, the fronts and all those things that will give the app its final look and feel. This stage is all about details and tests. At this stage, you cannot go back to objectives and design. You can only focus on the final inputs. However, this is a critical stage, where feedback is still needed to release an excellent final product. Remember, the team has already accomplished a lot, and the feedback needs to be positioned in a way that is useful and may not cause much rework. It's a good idea to give the project team overriding powers so that they can implement only areas of feedback that they think are useful.

By following the 70:20:10 method, you will find that not only is there less stress in the team, but the team members gradually start looking at feedback as a positive enabler and something that aids their work and gives a better output. The method calls for some discipline and rules, but you will find that it's well worth it.

November Rain: Improving Through Sharing Feedback

As the team I was leading grew, two questions emerged:

1. How does each team member perceive the others in the team, both in terms of their individual competence and their collaboration with others?
2. What does the team think of me as a manager, and which are the areas that they feel I could do better at?

The company's appraisal system was too formal and not frequent enough to give a useful response to the above two questions. As a team, we needed a process that was informal, trustworthy and psychologically safe, in addition to what the company ran as a performance evaluation system. We collectively came up with a process that worked well for the team. This process has stood the test of time and is in use even today. We labelled this process 'November Rain', mainly because it was launched in November and the rains that month, though cold and icy, are very useful for the land it rains on. Just as a true feedback system should be.

Any team can easily implement and use the November Rain feedback. At its basic level, it involves each team member rating others in the team as well as giving feedback to the manager. I have reproduced the launch email below, which will give you an idea of how it works.

Invitation Email to the Team

Dear Team Member,

As a team, learning and improving together has always been key to our success. As we come near the end of another interesting year, we are at the month where we tell each other how well we did and how we can do better next year. Your whole-hearted participation in this exercise will help all of to us improve and do better, both inside and outside of work. Constructive feedback increases self-awareness, clarifies behaviours, promotes dialogue, improves relationships and fosters a positive work environment.

This November, let us take feedback as a gift and help one another grow as individuals and help eliminate the stumbling blocks. Let us all take this feedback positively with a view of making room for improvement.

Attached is a spreadsheet with the names of all team members. The three columns are titled Partnering Score, Personal Effectiveness Score and Overall Score. You need to score each team member on each of these on a scale of 1–10 (10 being max). In addition, there are two columns kept for qualitative comments. An explanation about each column is mentioned in the spreadsheet in the form of a note. Below is a sample score for a peer.

Emp Name	Category	Partnering Score	Personal Effectiveness Score	Overall Score	You are great at	You could be better at/if...
ABC	Peer	7	8	7	Taking complete ownership of task, great to work with.	Making presentations to clients.

Similarly, you need to score for the names that appear on the spreadsheet (XLS). In case, you haven't interacted with someone in the team, you need not score them (hopefully this won't be many). You must include your manager in your feedback. Remember that your scoring scale should be consistent and fair. It's easy to remember this—score others in the same way as you would expect to be scored by them.

Some ground rules:

This is a trust and honour-based exercise.

Your input will be kept confidential and no feedback will be ascribed to an individual—return the filled-out sheet only to me.

You will not copy ratings and comments and fill in the XLS. Rating and comments need to be done with thought and be specific to the individual.

At the end of the exercise, I will send you the average scores and qualitative comments received for you as an individual. Remember, you will not receive your score or comments if you do not return the filled-out feedback form.
Aim to keep the feedback constructive, non-threatening and targeted at helping the individual improve. Any comment that is deemed harmful will be deleted.

Once I received the team's filled-out sheets, I would collate the scores and feedback received for each team member. I would then send out individual scores and feedback. The feedback was usually quite rich in terms of actionable inputs and team members did confirm to me that they found the exercise most useful and something they looked forward to doing every year.

For any feedback method to work, you need to create a safe space for your team. Both the Declining Feedback method and the November Rain exercise work well when team members trust each other and know that feedback is given with the right intent. Both the methods described in this section are structured to provide timely and useful feedback. The first one takes care of feedback for the work being done; the second one offers feedback to the individual. Both are simple, easy to implement and useful.

Building Empathy

Sometimes, as managers, we tend to be oblivious to the perspectives of our teams. To give you a better idea of what this means, let's look at an experiment that was conducted a while back in a college, in which teams of three students were assigned to work on a short project for three hours. Two students in the group were randomly assigned as team members and the third student was designated as the supervisor for the project. The supervisor was asked to evaluate the performance of the team members and determine their compensation. Around thirty minutes into the task, a plate of four cookies was placed in the room. It was interesting to see what happened to the spare cookie. Without fail, the student designated as the supervisor always ended up eating the extra cookie.

It shows that even a little power impacts the way people behave. If this can happen to students who are in the same class, think of what can happen in situations of actual power differentials, such as an office. People who have power over others become more focused on themselves and their needs and forget the needs of others, even thinking some rules don't apply to them.

Empathy is often described as the practice of putting yourself in someone else's shoes. It's not always possible to do this, as your team members or colleagues may go through varied life situations that are difficult to understand unless you have been impacted the same way. Some examples include the loss of a loved one, losing one's home to a wildfire, witnessing a loved one battle cancer, undergoing complex surgery and so on. While we may not be able to relate, we can always lead with empathy by showing compassion and care.

One of the things a manager can do in this situation is reduce or remove the workload of the person going through a tough time. Regardless of the circumstances impacting the employee, give them the space to breathe and not worry about work. For example, during the Covid-19 pandemic, people were struggling with multiple issues—childcare, parents stuck in a different city, personal illnesses and so on. At this point, people appreciated the managers who allowed them flexibility in their work. Employees returned the favour manifold by ensuring work completion at a favourable deadline and not letting the team down.

You can continue some of the practices that served us so well during the pandemic years of 2019–21, such as extended leave, remote working options and offering a day off to recharge mentally. All these options are well within a manager's purview. One of the things you should remember when working with your team is to separate productivity from presenteeism. As a manager, you don't need to micromanage the employee's way of working, you need to manage their work output.

Another example of leading with empathy is how to compassionately convey tough news, such as pay cuts or layoffs. Studies have shown that managers who convey the news with empathy and a sound explanation end up with better performance output and easier closures than managers who do not. Compassion can take many forms, but at its simplest, it means understanding what others are going through and being sincere in your approach. When delivering bad news, remember that you have more information than the person receiving it and you can filter how you present the good from the bad. How you treat people when they go through a difficult situation matters a lot. People will always remember how they were treated and whether it was fair. I have found that it's important to help people retain their dignity, which helps them see hope even in difficult times.

Towards Being a Better Manager

Being a better manager is about looking at incremental improvement in what you do. You may not realize this, but these small changes make a big difference to the team. Let's look at three important areas you can look at. By no means is this an extensive list, so you can add your own practices to make it work for you.

Optimizing resources: Often, managers are placed in situations where the team reports overwork. (In my experience, teams rarely report underwork, though office slacking does happen.) Overwork can happen due to several reasons—bad planning, sudden departure of a resource, a new technology introduced without training and so on. Overwork is bad for everyone in the team. The signs of overwork will be clear—spending late nights and weekends at the office, fatigue, missing personal commitments, low morale, etc. If your team is showing signs of overwork, it requires your immediate and direct intervention.

I once had an interesting conversation with a person who worked in my team and then moved on to a new manager. He was unhappy about how he had moved from a five-day work week to a six-day one, and his explanation caught my attention. He had calculated all the meetings that had been added to his calendar—direct meetings, meetings where he needed to participate despite not having any direct impact, follow-up meetings, team meetings, etc. These meetings added a total of eight hours and forty-five minutes to his weekly schedule. That equalled an extra day at work. It showed me how easy it is for a manager to add unproductive tasks to an employee's schedule. It's also equally easy to remove unwanted activities and give back time to your team. Doing this will work wonders for team morale.

Creating psychological safety: Have you ever had someone in your team tell you that something they tried did not work as expected? How do you handle such situations? Do you view them as learning exercises or do you take it out on the person who brought you the bad news? If it's the latter, you can be sure that bad news will travel very slowly to you in the future because there is low psychological safety in the team.

The concept of psychological safety comes from research conducted among teams working in hospitals.[4] The researchers found that teams that worked better together reported more surgical mistakes. This was contrary to the usual experience where teams hid their errors. The reason that some teams behaved differently was that the team collectively learnt from a mistake, and there was no fear of retaliation for being open about a mistake. These teams believed that it's acceptable to be transparent, to express their ideas and concerns, to speak up when needed and to admit mistakes—all without fear of negative consequences. These were labelled as teams that had high psychological safety.

Psychological safety is a team phenomenon—an emergent property of a team that works well together. The team sees it as their responsibility to speak up for the team's benefit. Irrespective of the profile of the company or the nature of the job, a team that has a higher level of psychological safety does better and is highly engaged. A manager has an important role to play in creating this environment, as their behaviour sets the tone for the rest of the team. Creating psychological safety doesn't mean being nice all the time; it's about being fair and kind. For creating a situation of psychological safety, it's important for the manager to lead by example, to be vulnerable and honest. By doing this, you are investing in your team's growth and development.

Providing predictability and regularity: There was an experiment conducted[5] during the London bombings (the Blitz) during World War II. Over time, the advance warning system about air raids became so accurate that the chances of a raid without the warning were negligible. Hence, people were able to go on with their work when the air raid sirens were silent. This helped maintain morale and gave the locals a sense of normalcy during a difficult period. The study found that if a stressful event could be predicted in advance, people would not need to maintain a state of constant vigilance and anxiety, which helped them handle the stressful event better.

The same holds true for organizational shocks, such as layoffs or closures due to a change in business circumstances. If the manager or leader can explain to people what is likely to happen and how long it will last, they will be better prepared. For example, some companies make an open commitment that there will be no further cuts in manpower for six months or that the current organizational structure will remain the same for the coming year. Having predictability helps people handle difficult situations better.

What if You Have to Work for a Toxic Boss?

Discussions on online job forums indicate an increase in the reporting of bad bosses.[6] However, it is unclear whether the increase is due to better reporting or a rise in the managerial pool. But what is clear is that the chances that you will encounter a bad boss sometime in your career are higher. Not everyone with a bad boss can quit their job and there is no guarantee you won't run into another Mr Hyde in your next one. So, let's explore some methods of dealing with a bad boss.

Create boundaries: This might sound counterintuitive, but having a clear expectation and boundary for every interaction helps you respond better to a toxic supervisor. The idea is to keep the relationship strictly professional, so if you set clear boundaries and rules of engagement, you will find that the interactions become tolerable and you now have time to focus on things that matter. For example, you can specify that you will deliver a given task by a certain time and you will not get any stressful follow-ups. As you continue to stick to your commitments, your time and boundaries will be respected.

Define your job and deliver: It's very important to seek clarity on the job expectations and be clear in your communication. It's a good practice to provide regular updates on a task discussion and its progress. There might be varied management styles, and all you need to do is be clear about the objectives, work towards them and check your ego at the door. The last part is not easy but remember that you are more than your workplace.

Build a mentoring pool: Most workplaces have a mix of good and bad managers. It's useful to be aware and tap into the larger managerial pool that is available. You could seek advice through conversations with other managers and maybe even change a few things with their help. Be careful not to complain about your manager but convey to the organization that you are dealing with a bad manager through the process of mentoring. A strong support network is especially useful when dealing with challenging managers. Having access to people who can support and encourage you provides you with an outlet and possibly even an alternate job.

Have positive conversations: While it may not be easy to engage in conversations with difficult managers, you can try to have some at periodic intervals. These conversations will help you put across your concerns and queries, and you should continue them even if they don't go the way you want.

Adapt and check: One necessary action is to assess your own personal values. We can't always control the office environment. However, you can control how you react to the environment. As long as your objective does not clash with your personal values, you can adapt to the environment. Treat this as an interlude on your career journey and don't take your manager's actions or comments personally.

Results matter: Finally, what you produce matters. Focus on your objective and deliver beyond expectations. Make the results known to others who matter. If you shift your mindset to delivering what is outlined, the toxic manager can only do that much damage. Rather than complaining about your bowling or the pitch, focus on improving your game.

Finally, What about Those Who Are Not Managers?

Finally, we should be aware that toxic workplaces happen due to the actions of both toxic employees and toxic managers.[7] These are people you should try to avoid because they are disruptive, spread negativity and have low opinions about the company, its business and its leadership. They are also people who can't be reasoned with or changed with alternate points of view. When given an opportunity, they exhibit bad behaviour, put down colleagues and disrupt morale in the workplace. They do not necessarily spread toxicity in an abrasive manner. Many of these employees are good to interact with on the surface, but they sow seeds of disruption in a way you won't even realize.

Bob Sutton is a renowned Stanford professor who teaches engineering and management. Around twenty years ago, Prof. Sutton came up with the theory that so-called 'office assholes'[8] (OAs) weren't just a nuisance; they also cost the company money through their bad behaviour through attrition and other productivity losses. As a leader, it is your job to identify these toxic employees and get rid of them quickly. Equally pertinent is having a self-awareness mechanism to prevent you from turning into one in the future.

A simple way to keep your office clear of such toxic employees is to enforce a 'no OA role'. The person you want in your team might be an absolute star but they have a reputation for bad behaviour. This does not mean you should only hire nice people who fit in, but you need to determine whether someone is simply a tough cookie or a potential problem.

Let's look at some of the characteristics of OAs.

Do they take joy away from an interaction every time you meet?: Do you feel oppressed, humiliated, de-energized or belittled when you talk to them? Do you feel worse about yourself after the discussion than before? Also, it's possible that this person behaves differently based on your position in the organizational structure. He behaves better with those above him and directs venom at people who are less powerful.

Common signs to watch out for: There are many ways in which OAs will try and ply their trade. Some use personal insults; others make sarcasm their weapon of choice. Some of the commonly used tools in their tool kit are personal insults, threats and intimidation; sarcastic jokes; targeted emails with others marked on it; status reminders; public humiliation; rude interruptions; physical invasion of space; ignoring people and so on.

Someone has allowed them to behave this way: Typically, an OA has a patron from senior management or has now reached a level of seniority. They believe they are indispensable to the organization, which is largely due to the fact that the person is allowed to continue even when their team has high attrition and low morale.

Sadly, many organizations allow OAs to continue without realizing the damage they cause. Research shows that a negative interaction has a larger impact on morale than a positive one. Impacted employees may engage in defensive activities like resigning, falling sick or just doing just enough to get by. The higher the OA's position, the more damage it causes. Prof. Sutton's team has calculated the possible cost of an OA—for an organization of about 1000 people, the cost of one OA can be about $2 million in just replacement costs. In addition, sometimes companies end up settling lawsuits caused by the OA or paying compensatory damages. This is why organizations should apply the 'no OA' rule. When you commit to having this rule, you also commit to treating every employee with respect.

And once you have such a principle, you need to stick to it by demonstrating action. You cannot tolerate anyone behaving badly, no matter how senior or important they are. Even if you allow one OA to exist, you might as well say goodbye to the policy.

As organizations grow, they tend to add layers and become hierarchical. This leads to power differentials, and when people perceive themselves as having a higher status, they sometimes tend to behave badly by viewing others as a little lower and taking credit for things they did not do. One of the things you need to do as a leader is reduce the differences between employees. Some of the ways you can do this are by not creating a hierarchy-led benefit like reserved parking, separate dining rooms, etc. Another is by improving the performance management process to accurately connect work to rewards.

It's important to differentiate the OA from the difficult or argumentative office worker. The latter is needed to keep a check on group thinking and present an alternate view. As long as facts are used as the basis for decision-making, it's all right to allow anyone to bring a contrary view or challenge decisions. It's good to encourage this practice as it improves the quality of output. There are many businesses that did not survive in a competitive environment because people avoided asking difficult questions.

If you know who the toxic employees are, you can be proactive about solving this before letting the toxicity affect you. Here are some of the things you can do to counter OAs:

Take bad behaviour head on: Regardless of what the issue is, you should act the right way to correct the behaviour or remove yourself from the situation. As much as possible, do this in a way that allows for honest communication while maintaining boundaries.

Use company provided resources: Document everything and seek HR assistance. To protect your interests, you should detail the incidents so that HR can take steps to address the behaviour. It's also important to note your actions so the facts are clear to a neutral observer. Check your HR department's process and reputation for supporting employee grievances. Discuss with them the issues you are facing and see if they can provide you with a solution to rectify the situation. They might already be aware of the issue and have made a plan, as others might have come to them before.

Create a positive space for yourself: When it comes to workspaces, it is possible to create a space for yourself that is free from the influence of toxic people. Ensure you have outlets outside of work for socializing and reducing stress. Talk to a coach, a therapist or other trained professionals.

* * *

In this chapter, we have covered different positions that you can find yourself in with a team member, a manager or a leader. Some of the principles are interchangeable. We all have examples of people we would rather not have around because of the effect they have on us. It's equally important for us to not become one of such examples ourselves, either at work or in our personal lives. I had a manager many years ago who had this sign in his room that read, 'Everyone who enters this room brings joy to it, some when they enter, others when they leave.' As far as possible, try to put yourself in the first category.

You should divide the people in your life into three main groups: your inner circle, whom you trust and who will lift you up; the ones who have a positive influence on you, like your mentors or advisors; and the last category, others. You would have carefully filled in the first two categories. Now do the same with the last category by avoiding people who are a negative influence and leaving only those who bring joy.

You do not need to fully cut off people, as that may not always be a realistic solution. This is where setting boundaries comes in. Limit your interaction to the essential. Remember, we have energy exchanges every day—at home, at our workplace and more recently, over social media. These energy exchanges alter our mood and thinking and take us away from what we want to do during the day. We need to create boundaries with people who can drain us of our energy.

Every interaction can either bring joy (positivity) or drain joy (negativity). The choice remains with us. If nothing good or productive can come out of an interaction, run away. The most powerful word you have in your arsenal is 'NO'. Let it be your power wand; use it as needed when it comes to interaction and people. Saying no to someone isn't rude; it just helps you set boundaries for relationships and gives you mental peace.

Chapter 4

Embracing Tomorrow: Rediscovering Health for a Fulfilling Life

Sufficient sleep, exercise, healthy food, friendship and peace of mind are necessities, not luxuries.

—Mark Halperin

In the many years I have spent in human resources, I cannot forget the incidents that involved young people landing up in emergency rooms due to a health crisis, which they could have avoided had they paid better attention to their well-being. There is no tragedy greater than a life not fully lived. While some emergencies were caused by accidents or other things beyond one's control, a good number were caused by health situations, such as cardiac disease or stroke. In my early days as an HR manager, I remember accompanying a twenty-six-year-old employee to the hospital. He had suffered a sudden cardiac arrest while at work and collapsed. Sadly, despite all efforts, he did not make it. When his medical reports were shown to his family, the doctor explained that he had the cardiovascular profile of someone twice his age. It seemed like he had given up half of his life because of poor lifestyle choices.

The demands of a modern workplace can impact our health and well-being, both physical and mental. As we rise in our careers, these impacts accumulate. By the time we find out, many times it ends up being too late to reverse the situation. The good news is that with some conscious effort, we can balance our work and lifestyle, build relationships with friends and loved ones and prevent health crises caused by our work–life choices.

An employer's responsibility towards employee well-being has more to do with overall parameters, such as work hours, workplace safety, good lighting and clean air and water. Good employers also look at fixing factors that can lead to ill health, both physical and mental. However, the ultimate responsibility for our well-being lies with us and not anyone else.

The best time to focus on health and a work–life balance is at the start of one's career. The second-best time to do this is today. No matter what stage of your career you are at, you can make a difference.

During the early phase of our careers, we find fulfilment in working long hours. Our effort leads to rewards, recognition and more work coming our way. Soon, you will find that activities and interests outside of work become less important and eventually recede into the background. Long hours at work will also result in consuming food from the cafeteria or vending machine. You might have a young family that needs your attention, but you will end up missing important occasions like an anniversary or your child's sporting event because of demands from your workplace. You think to yourself that you will make it up somehow, but once a routine sets in, it's difficult to come out of it.

Back in the 1950s, American psychologist Dr Abraham Maslow wrote the following: 'Life moves so much more rapidly now than it ever did before . . . the huge acceleration in the rate of growth of facts, of knowledge, of techniques, of inventions, of advances in technology . . . we need a different type of human being . . . who is comfortable with change, who enjoys change.'[1] What Dr Maslow left out was that adapting to the demands of the modern workplace will also require a change in our approach that takes care of our health and well-being.

We can visualize several shifts that are going to take place over the next few years due to advancements in technology and work models. We will see a shift from fixed work hours to flexible continuous hours, a shift from physical activity to one that is more mental and sedentary, and a shift in our nutrition patterns, among others.

When we start our careers, we have a vision of where we would like to reach or the goals we would like to accomplish. We are usually inspired and committed to making this happen. At the same time, we need to visualize where we would like to be in terms of our health, family and life goals. Both work and life goals need to be congruent and managed. We will explore some ideas for how we can do this.

Balance Begins with the Work Week

Let's begin by balancing our work week. A day is too short with varying demands, whereas a month is too long. The week is perfect, as it has seven days, including the weekend. The idea is that if we can achieve a balanced work week, we can expand the same to the month and the year by following the same plan. We will focus on all the components that are important for work–life balance and see how we can focus on each through the week.

- Work
- Health
- Family / Friends
- Hobbies / Play
- Rest / Sleep

You could spend varying amounts of time on each dimension. For example, you might spend more time at work from Monday to Friday and indulge in your hobbies on Saturday. However, the time you spend on health and sleep needs to be consistent throughout the week. When we look at 'balance' it means being conscious of all the components that are important for us and ensuring we don't focus on only some and neglect the others.

Work

In the 1940s, the average worker put in a far higher number of hours than the worker today. Regulations like the Fair Labor Standards Act (FLSA) in the United States and other similar legislation across the world brought down the number of hours worked per week to about 45 by the 1980s. Across the world, people settled on a reasonable 9 a.m. to 5 p.m. schedule where the whole office started the day at the same time in the morning and ended it at sunset. While there were some exceptions and overtime, this work pattern gave people enough time for leisure and exercise.

In the early 2000s, new workplace technologies allowed people to access work-related information on handheld devices. This made anytime work possible, and out went the concept of fixed hours and undisturbed leisure time. In the last few years, pervasive work technology has expanded exponentially, mainly aided by the investments made during the pandemic. Now you could be doing a video conference call at midnight from your bedroom, and it's become difficult to draw a line between work, home and leisure time. An added problem is the culture of 'presenteeism' wherein missing such late-night meetings may lead to you being regarded as someone who is not fully committed to work.

Using our work week measure, the first thing you need to do is have a weekly task schedule that helps you plan the week. Having a weekly plan helps you manage your time as well as reduce stress due to unfinished work at the end of the week. When you plan your week, you need to build in some slack, as there will be some unanticipated additions or a shift in priorities. Your weekly work plan becomes the starting point, with about 30 per cent flexibility for adjustments. A weekly plan works best when you use it consistently. Do not stop using it because a particular week or two did not go as per plan.

Now, let's look at how to create a weekly work plan and get the most out of it.

The first step is to have clear ideas of your goals for the month or quarter, and then work out what you want to accomplish towards the goals on a weekly basis. Imagine that the week is like an empty jar. You need to put the bigger pieces in first. Those are your long-term objectives. The rest of the jar (week) can be filled with smaller tasks, followed by sand, representing the trivial tasks. You might even need to accommodate some of the tasks you couldn't finish. Calculate the total amount of time you have budgeted for the week. It should not cross thirty-five hours, as the rest is for slack. If your count of hours is greater than thirty-five, you need to remove some of the items in the jar.

Next, follow a routine to plan your week. I find that using Fridays to plan ahead helps. Some of my friends do their planning on Sunday. Both have their benefits: Friday allows you two days of the weekend to think and reflect, and Sunday allows you to build in what has been added over the weekend. Either way, a routine is important. Once you have a planning routine, stick to it.

Once you have planned for the week, it's important to plan and balance the individual days based on the schedule. If you have a task that needs focus, you might want to do it on a day that has fewer meetings. You might use the busy days to get some light tasks on your list completed. When working through your task list for the day, plan for breaks. Some of these breaks are good to focus on the other dimensions of work life. For example, taking time out after a heavy task is a good time to fill in some exercise. Francesco Cirillo, a university student, developed an interesting technique that I have found useful. It is called the Pomodoro method.[2] He tweaked his study schedule to arrive at an optimal one. It consisted of working for twenty-five minutes with a five-minute break, then repeating this schedule. After every four such cycles of a total time of two hours, you take a cumulative fifteen-minute break. Once you get used to this schedule, you can figure out how many twenty-five-minute cycles you will need for a task and plan your day accordingly.

Don't forget to plan for two important aspects of the work week. If you are someone who works in an office for five days, you would be adding commute time unless you live close by to the office. If you have some work-from-home days, you will have some additional time on those days that you can use productively. Using a weekly work plan helps you stay organized, reduce your stress level, manage your tasks and give you a sense of accomplishment. You will find that with a little bit of planning, the dread of Mondays will decrease, and you will be better able to focus on other areas of work–life that are important.

If you are a team leader or manager, you could schedule the work week for the entire team by creating a shared schedule. This can help the team prioritize, clear bottlenecks due to dependencies and ensure the project runs smoothly. The entire team can have visibility into the shared work as well as plan their individual work weeks better.

The office automation tools to manage work weeks are evolving rapidly. There are enough tools, AI-enabled or otherwise, in the open domain that you can use. For example, there are tools that can pull out all the pending tasks by analysing your calendar and email inbox and preparing a preliminary task list for the week. The tool can even generate a weekly work plan and track progress. So many manual tasks can now be automated. It still needs you to analyse and arrive at a final schedule, but it doesn't need the time that was needed in the past. Once you are comfortable with a planning tool, incorporate it into your planning activity.

A productive work week is not about the number of hours you spend at work. It's about being efficient, knowing your body and the signals it sends and knowing when to stop working. It's about learning to set boundaries in a seamless manner so that both aspects are given the attention they need. This needs some planning and practice to get right, especially that routine that works for you as an individual. Once done, it will free up your mind and allow you to focus on other areas of work–life.

Health

Maintaining one's health requires a balanced diet, regular exercise, sufficient sleep and stress management. Additionally, staying hydrated and avoiding harmful habits, such as smoking, help keep you healthy. One of the effects of modern office work is that it encourages physical inactivity and calorie-rich diets accompanied by stress and anxiety. This will cause us to become unhealthy over time.

Let's look at some simple things we can do to maintain our health. This section is not meant to be a detailed guide, but rather a summary of essential considerations. There are plenty of resources, both online and offline, that can give you more details and help you tailor your individual health plan.

The first step is to keep track of your diet. When we work, we tend to not focus on the calories we consume or the type of food we eat. Over time, this becomes a habit that is difficult to change. The goal is to have a diet that is balanced and nutritious and is in line with your activities at work. You can consult a nutritionist at your office health facility or work out your dietary needs on your own. Once you have worked out what works best for you, stick to the diet as much as possible. Limit unhealthy food and stick to your meal schedule. Don't forget to have three meals a day with a balance of protein and fibre that are low on fat, sugar and calories. Look at foods that are low on the glycaemic index, a measure of sugar in the food. As sugar is the main stimulus for insulin secretion, these foods promote high fat and cholesterol levels and store excess nutrients as fat in the body.

Secondly, drink water regularly to stay healthy. As humans, we need water to aid in breathing, filter waste and for digestion. In fact, 65 per cent of our body's cellular mass is water. Drinking water is still the cheapest and best way to stay hydrated, as opposed to any other beverage choices. However, if you are involved in heavy physical exertion, or lose fluids owing to an illness, you might need oral rehydration salts (ORS). These are available off-the-counter (OTC) in most pharmacies, so keep them handy if you are working in extreme heat and humidity.

Exercise regularly and stay active. Whether it's at-home workouts, yoga, cycling or simply walking the dog, being physically active is important. Reduce your sitting and screen time as much as possible. Being sedentary increases your risk of diabetes, heart disease and stroke. One of the advantages of modern workspaces is that they are designed with the ability for people to move around. Make full use of the time you are in the office to get some walking done while at work and take the stairs if you can. Simple changes to your commute, such as walking home from the metro station or getting off one bus stop earlier, can contribute to your health without impacting your schedule too much.

Go easy on intoxicants. You will be invited to office gatherings where alcohol is served. An occasional drink is fine, but don't forget that alcohol has empty calories that add up very quickly. The rule about alcohol is to always consume it in moderation. Alcohol causes significant water and mineral losses and is also calorific dense.

Take vitamin supplements on a regular basis, based on your doctor's advice. While most of your requirements for vitamins and minerals needed for a healthy body will come from your diet, you may not get everything your body needs from the food you consume, so supplements can help here.

Take care of your mental health. It's common to have feelings of fear, anxiety, etc. While there is a shift towards greater mental health awareness, there is still psychological suffering and trauma due to burnout and other issues at the workplace. If you feel that you cannot deal with your mental health on your own, do reach out to employer provided resources or seek professional help.

Note: These are general health tips intended for informational purposes. Please consult your doctor or a health professional before you arrive at a health routine that works for you.

Family and Friends

Human beings do not perform at their best when alone. Having supportive family and friends serves as a pillar of support and can positively impact our health. Emotional connections, shared responsibilities and a strong support system contribute to both physical and mental well-being. Social connections are linked to lower stress levels and improved mental health, which, in turn, can have positive effects on physical health. Studies have shown that having supportive relationships is a strong protective factor against falling ill.[3]

However, we must exercise caution and establish meaningful relationships with a select few people in our network, rather than having too many friends and shallow relationships that may be toxic. Focus on building and maintaining a small group of people that you can trust and who will be there to support you and who you can lean on during times of difficulty.

As humans, we have basic physiological needs and after that, come our social needs. Having a sense of belonging to a larger group is something that has been ingrained in us since the time our ancestors dwelled in caves. Just like it takes a village to raise a child, it takes a larger group of well-meaning people to develop a successful professional.

It's important to have a diverse group of people around you, as they will be able to bring out different perspectives that will be useful. For example, a friend who is open to taking risks might push us towards a career decision that would be right for us, but we may be scared to take the leap on our own. A quiet friend might give us space and listen to what is bothering us. Having a friend at work can be the best thing that can happen to you. Friendships play a significant role in our overall well-being. Friends provide emotional support, companionship and a sense of belonging. Positive social interactions contribute to mental and emotional resilience. Cultivating and maintaining meaningful friendships can positively impact your quality of life.

Workplaces can be difficult places. Without a friend to share your day with, a workplace can be deary, and the usual everyday stresses and unpleasant experiences can negate the positive ones. People who have friends at work consider going to work a positive experience. You would tend to see fewer examples of burnout in this group, and they would generally be more productive and happier. Surveys reinforce this. According to the 2021 Workplace Friendship & Happiness Survey[4] by Wildgoose, 57 per cent of people say having a best friend in the workplace makes work more enjoyable, 22 per cent feel more productive with friends and 21 per cent say friendship makes them more creative.

One of the observations from the remote work phase during the pandemic was the loss of connection with fellow colleagues. Friendships reduced as it was difficult to maintain those in a remote or hybrid world. Some friendships do transcend the office, but most are dependent on them to make them work. Companies can contribute to fostering work friendships by creating an inclusive workplace environment. I have some managers whose teams have very close bonding, and they make regular attempts to create connections beyond work.

Starting and developing work friendships can't be forced, but there are some things you can do:

i. Create opportunities for human conversations: I have found going out with team members for long walks most useful. It lets you have conversations at a leisurely pace and also adds to your health goals.
ii. Personal lives: While there is a threshold that you should not cross, having an interest in the lives of your teammates beyond work and connecting with them on a personal level helps.
iii. Celebrate success: Work can be made so much more interesting by celebrating things that ought to be celebrated. A birthday, a work anniversary, someone closing a sale and so on. Look for opportunities to celebrate.
iv. One of the practices you should keep active is being in regular touch with your networks. This needs effort and conscious attention. Annual greetings for Diwali or New Year don't make the cut. If you are one of those spontaneous people who can be in regular touch, then you are lucky. Most others need to make a conscious effort. By putting in time and effort to maintain your relationships, you will be sure that your network will be there when you need it.

Hobbies and Play

Hobbies provide a means of relaxation, stress reduction and mental simulation. They offer an outlet for creativity and personal expression, promoting a sense of accomplishment and fulfilment. Participating in activities that are enjoyable can positively impact mood and overall well-being. Incorporate hobbies into your work week rather than pursue them in your spare time to serve as conversation starters. Hobbies have a big impact on overall mental health and well-being.

Hobbies are part of the 360-degree approach to work–life balance and give you a break from the demands of work. Having something different to do can recharge you both mentally and physically. Depending on what your hobby is, it may add to your network or profile. Those who have fulfilling hobbies are less likely to suffer from burnout and exhaustion. Hobbies require us to learn new skills, challenge ourselves and go beyond the normal.

Finding a hobby can be easy or hard. Try and choose something that helps you grow as an individual, learn new skills and challenge yourself. Some examples are learning a new sport or musical instrument; engaging in physical activities such as swimming, running or yoga; doing something for underprivileged kids like teaching in a local school, etc. Go ahead and choose anything that will sustain your interest over time.

Your hobby could also give you a sense of accomplishment that your regular work may not be able to provide. You will find that winning the weekend cricket tournament will give you a high that will last for some time and have a positive impact on your work. As a leader, it's good to encourage employees to pursue hobbies by providing some flexibility and resources. These things usually don't cost much and make a big difference in creating a healthy workplace.

Incorporating a play routine, such as table tennis or chess, into the workday is valuable for mental health and a healthy lifestyle. Play is crucial for both children and adults. It contributes to cognitive, emotional and social development. Play can serve as a stress reliever, fostering creativity, improving relationships and promoting overall well-being.

In addition to the above, consider participating in sports outside of the office. Sports have a positive impact on well-being. They contribute to developing both physical skills and emotional skills. For example, winning and losing is something that happens every day on the sports field and helps you handle your office situations with a calmness that would otherwise be difficult.

When I was a child, we used to have long summer holidays and the children of the neighbourhood would gather at the local cricket field for several games throughout the day. Somehow, the summer heat and dusty environment never got in the way of happiness. Over the years, the local grounds have given way to buildings and children are missing out on a very important part of growing up. Outdoor games with friends have been replaced by sedentary activities, the biggest of which is web streaming. As a professional, you must deal with the double whammy of being sedentary at office and at home. This leads to obesity and other lifestyle illnesses. Being overweight increases the risk of chronic illnesses, including cardiovascular disease, hypertension and stroke, certain forms of cancer and type 2 diabetes, all of which result in a reduced quality of life. Involvement in sports can lead to better eating habits and healthier lifestyles.

Life is unpredictable at times, and the ability to adapt to change is an asset. Studies have demonstrated that physical exercise[5] improves attention span and boosts productivity. It makes sense, therefore, to incorporate exercise regimes into your work week. Choose a sport that you love—one that you have always wanted to learn to play. Call up a couple of friends and play a fun game outside. Experience the thrill that you have been missing out on by being stuck in the office all day. Come out and play.

Rest and Sleep

Getting a good night's sleep has an important role to play in your long-term health. During sleep, your body repairs and rejuvenates itself so that you feel better when you are awake. On average, you need about seven hours of sleep a night. While this might vary a bit, those who go around claiming that four hours is adequate are not telling the truth. During sleep, your body is working to support healthy brain function and maintain your physical health. Over time, inadequate sleep can raise your risk of various health problems. It can also affect how well you think, react, work, learn, etc.

The sleep cycle is made up of two types of sleep: rapid eye movement (REM) sleep, where the brain is more active and we are more inclined to dream, and non-REM sleep, where the brain is quieter and slows down. You need both types of sleep, and if you sleep long enough, you will get adequate cycles of both. Your body also makes and releases hormones in tune with your sleep cycle that help you feel awake or sleepy depending on the time of the day. Sleep aids in learning and long-term memory formation. Not getting enough sleep, or not getting enough high-quality sleep, can lead to varied health problems.

Just like in the other areas we have seen, it's important to plan your sleep. Choose a quiet room with minimal light and stay away from phones and other screens. Light, especially the one emitted by electronic screens, has a poor impact on our sleep. The room should be well ventilated and have a pleasant temperature. As far as possible, keep your sleep and wake-up timings consistent.

Travel, particularly international travel across time zones, is another aspect that affects sleep. Give your body time to adjust to the new time zone. The best way to adjust is by setting your mental clock to work in the new zone. Meaning you go to sleep and wake up in the new time zone. Apart from this, hydrate yourself and get as much sunlight as possible during the day. You will find that doing this helps you cope much better.

Flourish, Don't Languish

About a year ago, a colleague came to me with a situation she was facing. At first, I didn't recognize the issue she was facing. She was having trouble concentrating at work. She was not excited about the new task of meeting people. She said that her leisure was primarily consuming vast quantities of online content while lying in bed, often till the early hours of the morning.

Without getting too deep into the science, it appears that what she was experiencing is a condition that is affecting people worldwide. It's been termed as 'languishing'. Languishing is a sense of stagnation and emptiness. It feels as if you're muddling through your days, without direction or visibility into the future.[6]

We talked through possible solutions to her problem and came up with a set of actions. I have reproduced them below, as they are useful irrespective of whether you are going through a situation like hers or want to avoid one in the future.

Physical Exercise

My colleague started an exercise routine. She started walking more and counted her steps on her phone. Having a tracker encouraged her to do more, and she came up with simple ways of increasing her step count, such as walking across the office to meet a colleague or parking away from the mall entrance. Once she established a regular walking routine, she incorporated some additional exercises that could be done anywhere. Push-ups, low-intensity jogging, skipping rope and so on.

Exercise has consistently been shown to be a powerful mood booster and regulator. If signing up for a new gym class motivates you to move, do it. Find something that works for you—walking the dog, climbing stairs at the office, desk yoga, anything. You will find that even small doses of physical activity and low-impact exercise make you feel better.

'Flow' for Mental Exercise

The second thing my colleague discovered was that she was at her best when occupied with work or a task. She liked what she called 'being in the flow'. In addition to seeking challenging tasks for her work assignment, she created tasks for herself. She would start her mornings by solving the popular *New York Times* Wordle puzzle for the day. She started learning to play the guitar in the evenings.

Finding new challenges, enjoyable experiences and meaningful work are all possible remedies to languishing. In addition to 'flow', you can also add meditation to your mental health routine. It's one of the easiest things to do to maintain your mental health and can be done anywhere, anytime. You can introduce meditation into your regular routine, for example, before a presentation or a difficult meeting, or during your commute. You will find that you are able to perform better at work and stay calm while handling difficult situations.

Focusing on Small Goals

My colleague decided to focus on small wins. These small steps helped her rediscover the energy and enthusiasm that she was known for. If some days turned out differently, she gave herself permission to call them break days and enjoy them. That took away the pressure and allowed her to run her plan long-term.

Crafting Your Own Wellness Programme

It is good to have a wellness programme tailored to your own needs. The reasons are simple—a regular plan does two things. It ensures you stick to a schedule for routine check-ups by a professional and also keeps you on track to stay healthy through the year. There is clear evidence of a higher prevalence of what are termed lifestyle diseases—diabetes, hypertension, cardiac events and stress-related mental issues. The challenge with many lifestyle diseases is that they are not tangible; hence, they are also referred to as 'silent killers'. Some of the signs might be obvious, such as weight around the waist, breathlessness while climbing stairs, lack of focus at work, disturbed sleep, etc. But often, it's not so obvious and having a programme helps.

Many companies offer various health and wellness programmes, ranging from preventive health check-ups to office facilities like gyms and regular yoga or Zumba classes. You can build your programme around what the office offers or create your own. But it's important that you have a personalized health and wellness plan.

Here are the main components to include in your wellness programme. You can draw on what works best for you in consultation with your doctor or a health professional.

1. Annual medical check-up.
2. A plan for physical exercise.
3. Overall health assessment, including a check for mental well-being.

Annual Medical Check-Up

An annual medical check-up is like scheduled maintenance for your car or bike. It provides you with insights about your body's condition and recommends lifestyle adjustments or treatment plans, if necessary. Health check-ups usually suggest small changes to your lifestyle, but sometimes they do find indications of illness and help you seek treatment.

A usual health check-up includes the following and is usually done once a year. But there can be variations, and your doctor is the best person to guide you. Many hospitals offer routine health checks that include a doctor's consultation. You can opt for a hospital-provided health check if it's convenient.

A basic blood profile: routine blood count to measure the main blood cells like RBC, WBC, platelets and haemoglobin.

A blood lipid profile: these are tests for measuring levels of fat and, thereby, risk for cardiac disease. Typical measures are high-density lipoprotein

(HDL), low-density lipoprotein (LDL), triglycerides and total cholesterol.

Diabetes: Glycated haemoglobin (HbA1c), fasting blood sugar and random blood sugar.

There might be other tests that measure thyroid function, liver function, mineral composition, electrolyte composition and so on. These are usually optional and prescribed by a doctor based on specific symptoms.

Treadmill test: This is one of the most common tests to check for cardiovascular health. It involves walking on a treadmill or a stationary exercise bike while you are hooked to a cardiac monitor that shows your heart activity. This test determines how well your heart responds during the time when it is working hardest.

Cancer screening: If you are over the age of forty, it is recommended to go for cancer screening once every two years after consulting your doctor.

Physical test: weight, body mass index and general appearance.

Dental check: for any dental issues like cavities, gum disease, etc. It can be scheduled separately with your dentist.

Note: The information above is not to be considered medical advice and it is not intended to replace consultation with a qualified medical professional.

* * *

Your health is one of the most important things in your life. It affects your physical, mental and emotional well-being. That's why it's so important to be proactive about your health and take steps to prevent illness and disease. Being proactive in your health means taking steps to improve your health before you get sick. This includes things like eating a healthy diet, exercising regularly, getting enough sleep, etc. It also means getting regular check-ups with your doctor and following some simple rules that will drive a better balance between work and life.

Chapter 5

Crafting Human Experiences at Work

I never viewed technology as a replacement for the human experience. I viewed it as something that could liberate the human experience.

—Sal Khan

In a small village located high in the Swiss Alps, there is a family-run restaurant that is so popular that it's difficult to get a table on most days. This restaurant is small, doesn't advertise and doesn't have a Michelin star. It's not featured in travel or food blogs either. You reach the restaurant after driving through a very scenic mountain road, and the crisp alpine air has already worked up your appetite. You are welcomed by the friendly staff, who greet you by your name and seat you at your table with the minimum fuss. They make you feel like you are entering their home as a guest. Once you are comfortably seated in the dining area overlooking a beautiful valley, you are invited to go through the menu of the day. Despite the limited choices, each item is prepared with care. You can sense the efficiency and warmth of the hospitality throughout your meal. Your glass is topped at the right time, the service is attentive but not intrusive and you enjoy a delicious meal in a relaxed environment.

While there are many fine dining restaurants around the world, I have yet to come across one that has stayed in my memory for the experience. The meal we had during our visit was not expensive, the ingredients were fresh and locally sourced and the experience was exceptional without being over the top.

We crave experiences that make us feel human and this is relevant in the workplace too. Much of our pleasure and association come from travel, dining, work, entertainment, etc. The experiences that stay with us are simple—the dew on the grass on a winter morning, the colours of fall, an interaction with a friend over coffee, the visit to a new country, our first day at work, etc. Experiences are part of being human, whether they involve relationships, objects, interactions or places. These experiences shape our understanding of the world and our place within it. The human experience is a combination of all the physical, cognitive, social, cultural and emotional experiences we go through.

In a similar way, our experience at work matters. Over the years, we have realized that employee experience has a great impact on their satisfaction and, in turn, happy employees offer customers a better experience. The staff at the Swiss restaurant were able to offer us a great experience because they took pleasure in their jobs and wanted us to experience the same delight with our meal. However, figuring out how to deliver the same experience to employees requires thought and effort. Human experience is the complete experience an employee has with the company. It starts from the way employees are treated during the recruitment process, to the state of the facilities, to the way fairness is exhibited and many other aspects of work that deeply touch them. It's the collective experience that an employee gets and how much of that makes them feel more human than one more resource at work.

Businesses around the world are investing in developing customer experiences that are close to being magical. When you compare the money spent on creating customer experiences to the amount spent on employees, it does seem disproportional. However, providing a better experience is not all about money; it's about doing the right things for employees and doing them consistently.

Let's look at how to improve the employee experience for all of us at work. It needs participation from employees, managers and the company.

Creating Mutual Trust

In November 2023, an under-construction tunnel collapsed in the northern Indian state of Uttarakhand, trapping the construction workers inside. Every kind of high-tech tool and method was used in consultation with experts in an attempt to rescue the trapped workers. But after days of attempts, it wasn't technology that brought success, but a team of so-called rat miners practising a craft that's officially illegal. This team burrowed through the mountain manually with great risk to themselves. When asked, the leader of the team said that in their profession, the team is family and the trust they have in each other is immense. They were willing to literally place their lives in their teammates' hands.

There are two kinds of trust at play in any office. At the first level, there is the employees' trust in the organization and the organization's trust in its employees. At the next level comes the trust that a team has among its members. To gauge the trust that exists in your team, you just need to find the answer to a simple question. If one person on your team is unable to attend work for a few days during a busy time at work, will the rest of the team quickly rally around to finish his tasks or would they call out the lack of resources and leave things unfinished?

Mutual trust results in team empowerment. It demonstrates confidence in team leadership and in each other. Trust also motivates employees, promotes creativity and collaboration, improves retention and reduces risk aversion, all of which help the bottom line. You might have observed team empowerment at play stores and hotels, where employees needn't request special approvals to solve basic customer problems. At some hotels, staff can spend up to a reasonable limit without any approval to address guest issues.

One of the practices I observed in a well-performing team was that they had an email suggestion box for team members to drop notes about any processes that were impacting the team, along with their suggestions for change. At the end of the month, the suggestions would be anonymously put up for a vote by the other team members. The ideas that had merit needed to stand out on their own, and once voted, they were implemented. While this process did encounter initial hiccups, after a while, the suggestions got better and helped make work better for everyone. This simple action accomplished two things—it gave the team a sense of ownership and involvement in the daily work. Secondly, the idea's merit was unaffected by the identity of the messenger.

Closely related to trust is accountability, both the manager's accountability to the team and that of the team members to each other. On one level, accountability is about a willingness to ask questions and actively listen to the answers. It's not necessary for the person answering to always be the manager. It means that each person in the team must be clear about what they are working towards and help build a culture in which everyone understands that employee experience is a collective responsibility. A team completing its tasks without active supervision is a good measure of accountability.

Let's look at how we can build up the trust score at the place we work. There are four components that are integral to building trust among any team:

- **competence** or the ability to do the job
- **dependability** in terms of actually doing the job
- **humanness** in interactions with others on the job
- **transparency** in telling others the truth about the job

Of course, these four parameters don't cover everything, but they are a good assessment of workplace trust. A team can also be measured on these parameters to create a trust index for its members. For example, you could ask each team member to score the team on each of these four parameters and then average the scores to arrive at a team score. Once you have that, you could benchmark it with other teams as well as work on improving areas that don't score well.

Whenever you encounter an underperforming team, it's a good idea to look at its trust score. You don't even need a formal survey to do that. Discussions with team members will give you a good indication of the level of trust in the team. The best way to solve team trust issues is to put together a small group in the team and give them the responsibility of creating experiences on each of the above dimensions of competence, dependability, humanness and transparency. With active participation from the entire team, you can increase the trust score and make it a better experience at work for everyone in the team.

I have two examples of interventions that worked well during my time leading teams at Infosys. Once was about increasing team competence and the other was about humanness.

As a team, we had identified that we could increase the level of competence of team members through shared learning, done in a fun way. We put together a group of handpicked individuals who called themselves 'Trailblazers' and came up with several innovations around learning and competence building. One of their ideas was that by creating the right avenue for knowledge sharing, the team could leverage the expert knowledge each team member possessed in a certain area. Since they were given the freedom to experiment, they came up with very innovative solutions. Their ideas ranged from simple to complex. Thanks to the idea, the team could have book reviews and expert talk sessions; a formal tie-up with a business school for an online certification; podcasts on topics of interest and so on. They also kept the larger group regularly involved with fun activities like quizzes and other fun learning activities. The larger team greatly benefited from the learnings and increased their competence thanks to the 'Trailblazers'.

The next intervention was to do with increasing the 'humanness' quotient in the team. We realized we had people on the team with varying tenures. Some had just joined the team from business school; others had spent more than a decade in the same company. Considering the large team size, members would have different managers and have little reason to interact and share experiences. We wanted to increase the humanness quotient in the team by creating an opportunity for informal mentoring in both directions—the new team members and the older ones sharing ideas and interacting in a fun way. We worked on an initiative built around the concept of a neighbourhood. In any neighbourhood, you interact with different people, not just your family. These interactions contribute to your personal growth. You're probably familiar with the saying, 'It takes a village to raise a child.' We created multiple neighbourhoods in the office by bringing together a group of people who interacted on an informal basis on topics of interest. Some took on the role of mentors to aid the process and initiate the meetings, but largely the group was self-governing. We kept the group size within twenty-five to enable productive interactions. Team members who participated confirmed that they got to make new friends, build connections through a larger network and, above all, felt better in terms of the human experience.

In a similar fashion, you could design specific interventions to fix any of the four dimensions that contribute to the team's experience at work—competence, dependability, humanness and transparency.

Celebrating Success

It all started with an impossible idea. In the early years of Infosys, we had annual recognition awards that were presented at our head office in Bangalore. With a global workforce, not everyone could make it, and some got their awards through the office courier. One of the leaders threw up a challenge—could we use technology and link all our offices around the world? This way, the awardees could receive their recognition and their families and colleagues could watch it live and cheer them on. The technology for video conferencing was very primitive, presenting a tremendous coordination and technological challenge. Yet, when accomplished, it created a benchmark for celebrating success.

Celebrating an achievement with our team or marking a milestone like a work anniversary can be an amazing experience. We get so consumed with various things that demand our attention in the office that we sometimes forget to celebrate success. This includes our own success, as well as that of our team and friends. While it is right to assume that we need to focus on the larger goals at work, we do disservice to ourselves and our teams by ignoring moments of celebration. Appreciating each other and celebrating success costs very little. Recognition is a very cost-effective way to improve your work experience. People who are recognized regularly at work are always more engaged.

An opportunity for recognition and celebration can cover a wide set of things: the closure of difficult tasks, the achievement of job-related targets, performing a job to high standards, completing milestones, obtaining certifications and so on.

If needed, you can even create moments of celebration outside of workplace updates. In August 2023, I visited a workplace where big screens had been put up for employees to watch the lunar landing of Chandrayaan-3. The people in the office had nothing to do with the landing, but everyone felt good about celebrating the event, as they felt it was a shared success for all Indians. During the Covid-19 pandemic, when everyone was working out of their own homes, my team found that the middle of the week was the most difficult. So, they came out with a thirty-minute video call on Wednesday evenings where the whole team participated in a fun activity that was led by one of the team members chosen by rotation. In one memorable activity, each person shared something that brought them joy that week. At the end of that meeting, everyone was much happier after sharing joyful experiences. These Wednesday calls always had full attendance.

The next time you are watching a sport you like, observe how the players celebrate. It could be scoring a goal, winning a set or putting a hole. You will find that they put a lot of effort into their celebrations. While they each put in superhuman effort to get where they are, they also celebrate in a way that makes them feel fulfilled and rewarded for the many hours of hard work put in. A celebration serves to enhance awareness of what you have achieved and push you to further accomplishments.

Celebrating doesn't mean that you lose focus. In work situations where you are pressed to meet monthly and quarterly targets, you might have to consider the timing and duration of major celebrations. Dwelling on success for too long is a distraction and, worse, leads to complacency. Good teams know how to manage the balance between celebrating and looking forward to the next target. A good practice top performers and teams follow is that after each achievement, they make an effort to look not only at what worked but also at what went badly. This is best done in a team setting where the team splits up into small groups to identify and discuss both positive aspects of their performance and their scope to improve. The positive aspects are to be repeated; the other points need to be corrected as you move on to your next task. This simple exercise is a great way to build expertise and improve self-confidence.

One of the best examples of celebration that I have seen is when Infosys celebrated the milestone of achieving a billion dollars in revenue in 2004. Considering that this company started with a seed capital of only $200, this was a big achievement. The celebration included a concert by a popular entertainer, followed by a dinner. Each employee was gifted a commemorative digital watch. What truly took the experience to the next level was when every employee received a handsome bonus. I know that many people used it to buy TVs or home computers to commemorate this collective achievement. This company went on to achieve many more milestones, but the experience of that billion-dollar day is discussed by employees even now, twenty-odd years later.

Alignment of Values and Vision

One of the reasons people don't have a great experience at work is because of a misalignment between their personal values and the prevailing culture in their workplace. To put it simply, culture is a shared way of doing something with passion. If a company strives to uphold its core values in every employee interaction, whether it's recruitment, handling a project or evaluating performance, employees will see that they are part of a workplace that does the right things and they can share this passion to have a great experience at work.

Culture and shared values are important in a workplace because the stronger the culture, the less the bureaucracy. Everyone trusts everyone else to do the right thing at work. Families and tribes know this well—trust is ingrained and inherited by upcoming generations. You don't see them having a process manual to see who has to fetch water. If your company has heavy manuals and precise rules and procedures, it's also likely that you may not be getting a great human experience.

As an employee, you would want to align with the company's values, but in some situations, it's not fully clear what the values and vision is beyond the usual things said as part of corporate statements. Clear goals with well-defined milestones and success metrics connect employees to their company's mission and help them understand their role in advancing it. Ensuring employees are aligned with the company vision is a significant contributor to their experience at work. A company culture that supports a better experience understands the intrinsic connection between what it does internally for employees and how that translates into experiences.

Alignment is a major part of culture that starts even before employees join the company. One way to achieve this is through storytelling. People remember stories rather than statements and guidelines. If the leader explains to a new team why the company does certain things using stories, it is likely they will understand it better. When leaders tell stories, they drop the professional masks and demonstrate that they care. Storytelling humanizes both the narrator and the listener, resulting in a more positive human experience in the workplace.

Better Experiences through Technology

In January 2007, Steve Jobs took the stage in downtown San Francisco and told the eagerly awaiting audience that Apple was introducing three revolutionary products. 'The first one is a widescreen iPod with touch controls,' Jobs announced to a cheering audience. 'The second is a revolutionary mobile phone and the third is a breakthrough internet communications device. So, three things: a widescreen iPod with touch controls, a revolutionary mobile phone and a breakthrough internet communications device. 'An iPod, a phone and an internet communicator. An iPod, a phone . . . are you getting it?' he asked the audience. 'These are not separate devices. This is one device. And we are calling it iPhone.'

Steve Jobs cofounded Apple in his parents' garage in 1976, was ousted in 1985, returned in 1997 and by the time he died, in October 2011, had built it into the world's most valuable company. Along the way, he helped to transform the way we live and work by giving us a better experience through innovative technology. Today, you can use your phone to hail a cab to the airport, pay for your coffee at the terminal, know the status of your flight in real time, board the aircraft, entertain yourself in the air and, on landing, use it for a whole lot of new activities. Now, think of how your experience used to be before the smartphone was invented.

Imagine similar technology-enabled processes deployed at your workplace. You would experience a more professional, effective and personal interface. For example, technology could automatically connect you with a colleague who is working on something that could benefit from your expertise or your HR partner would proactively have information about your need to revisit your performance discussion with your manager. Once teething issues about privacy and data security are resolved, technology will enable better experiences for us at work, just as the launch of the iPhone triggered a customer experience revolution many years ago.

Sometimes, companies throw technology at people's processes in the hope that it will fix the deficiencies as well as give them better experiences. It does not quite work that way. You need to ideate on simplifying the process and technology in a way that makes sense for the user. The famous process consultant W. Edwards Deming put it beautifully almost forty years ago: 'Eighty-five percent of the reasons for failure are deficiencies in the systems and process, rather than the employee. The role of management is to change the process rather than badgering individuals to do better.'[1]

One of the frequent reasons for a bad employee experience is the sheer volume of applications an ordinary employee needs to navigate while at work. If the employee happens to be in the functions of HR, finance or procurement, this becomes even more acute. The amount of time the employee spends struggling with various discrete and non-integrated applications is considerable. We must start by designing our solutions in a human-centric way and view technology as not an end in itself but a tool for increasing productivity and reducing effort. Technology is one of the most poorly rated dimensions of the employee experience.[2] This is surprising, given the impact technology has had on our lives as customers. The main reason why technology at work gets a bad rating from employees is that it is complex and doesn't work seamlessly. The technology could range from collaborative tools, internal applications and service request desks to work devices and systems.

The technology used for the consumer experience is getting better because more attention is being devoted to it. Most companies work hard to reduce technology friction for customers but don't pay that much attention to the systems their employees use every day. I know from personal experience that employees spend more than a day just to log a travel request in the company system.

The same process on any commercial travel app would not take you more than five minutes. The result is reduced satisfaction and a terrible employee experience. We must ensure that both the customer experience and the employee experience get equal attention if we are going to improve the human experience at work. This can be done using an integrated human-centric approach while designing employee experience solutions. Once you shift to keeping the user at the centre and introduce technology around the user, the rest of the pieces will fall into place quickly.

Revitalize the Employee Experience at Moments of Truth

During the start of my career, I was in a sales role that required me to visit many workplaces, from factories to corporate offices. When you visit offices, you learn a lot from observation, especially how they provide different human experiences. Each workplace presented a different experience for the visitor. For example, some had a seamless visitor entry process. Others made sure to provide you with refreshments while you waited for your appointment or lunch after your discussion. My experience as a visitor and the impression I had of the company varied with how they handled what can be termed 'moments of truth'.

The concept of 'moments of truth' originated from customer experience research. It is usually defined as the defining point during a sale process where the customer decides to buy your product. There are usually multiple moments of truth in a sales journey. Similarly, moments of truth for an employee are the points that impact their experience with the organization. Companies that make the effort to identify the moments of truth at work are able to deliver a much better experience to employees. By identifying these points, you can then use technology or process design to provide better solutions.

Let's take the example of an employee using one of the most used processes—a leave application. You could treat all leave applications the same, just like many organizations do. When an employee fills out a form in the system, it goes to the manager for approval and if it is not approved within a certain time, it is automatically approved by the system. Now, let's assume that one of the applications is for parental leave. The system immediately highlights this fact to the manager and HR who then trigger a process that will ensure that the employee gets a personal call from the manager as well as a gift hamper with products for the newborn child delivered to their home. A moment of truth has been identified and is used to offer a better experience.

Another moment-of-truth experience for me was when I was interviewing for a position with Infosys in 2000, which was then a small company based out of Bangalore. While many parts of their recruitment process seemed ordinary, the experience they were able to give me when I visited the corporate office in Bangalore was the moment of truth. I remember this experience even twenty-five years later. From the security staff at the gate to the energetic lady manning the reception, as well as others I met over the course of the day, it clearly showed that this company had a human-first approach. In fact, by the end of the interview process, which went till late, a very senior person ensured that I had something to eat and was accompanied by the company transport that would drop me close to the city centre.

The human experience of an employee represents the collective experience that he or she has with the moments of truth while dealing with the organization. Human experience is driven by human centricity, which is the idea that people are much more than statistics or data. These experiences are driven by the emotions, needs and relationships that people experience when working for a company.

Let's look at how the hospitality industry approaches creating moments of truth for its guests. The hotel of tomorrow is going to be more digital and more personalized. Hotels are going to look at giving people choices between having shared experiences where they can interact and make friends and spaces where they can have a more private experience to rest and rejuvenate. This will be done in a way that is tailored to the needs of each guest.

The experience will start even before you check into the hotel, when you receive your reservation confirmation. A hotel focused on experience will ask you what would make you more comfortable and then ensure that you get what you want. For example, someone arriving from a long-haul flight would prefer to be in their room as quicky as possible, even perhaps ordering a light snack on the way from the airport and getting some sleep. Someone visiting the city for the first time might like input on places to visit and enjoy. And most importantly, if you are a repeat visitor, you would not like to go through the process of giving your preferences and filling out your data again. You would expect that they would be remembered.

The last part of creating great moments of truth is about empowering frontline staff. The front desk staff or restaurant staff in a hotel should be able to take immediate decisions to delight a guest without needing to go through multiple approvals. There is nothing that delights a guest as much as immediate action to remedy a situation.

Employees who experience positive moments of truth stay and those with bad ones re-evaluate their priorities and vote with their feet. Companies need to relearn what was once a given: their most valuable resource is their people.

The Five Daily Hassles to be Aware of at Work

The human experience at work has nothing to do with the organization, its processes or technology. It's also dependent on interaction with others at work. Human experiences in connection with others at work can be diverse and intricate. They involve the warmth of shared laughter, the comfort of understanding glances, the depth of intimate conversations, the resilience found in support during challenging times, the joy of shared achievements and the bittersweet nature of saying goodbye.

Experiences with people can be positive or negative. At work, it's natural that you are exposed to both positive and negative experiences while performing your job. Positive experiences would include a pat on the back from your manager for a job well done, welcoming a colleague back from maternity leave, etc. Negative experiences include a lack of manager support, unplanned tasks assigned in a hurry, annoying co-workers, etc. Both positive and negative experiences cause fluctuations in your emotional state and your ability to perform well at work.

Let's look at how we can increase our positive experiences and reduce negative experiences at work. We can do that by reducing our exposure to some of these common hassles we face at work.

1. **Conflicts and unpleasant interpersonal interactions:** These are disagreeable behaviours or situations

directed at you by your colleagues, managers, supervisors, or customers. These often involve aggressive communication, a lack of empathy and making you feel low as an individual.

2. **Time pressures and bad work tasks:** These are to do with difficulties in managing daily tasks and working on routine and unchallenging tasks.
3. **Performance pressures:** These stem from the constant evaluations and feelings of inadequacy in managing challenging tasks and situations.
4. **Failures, interruption and annoyances:** These are things that disturb your daily work and stop you from focusing.
5. **Organizational and leader-related hassles:** These involve organizational hurdles such as bad managers, bureaucratic rules, a poor workplace environment owing to a demeaning leader, vague work assignments, etc.

These are just broad categories. We are sure to encounter more as we progress in our work journey. The key is to recognize a potential hassle when you see it and remove yourself before it impacts your experience at work.

Measuring Human Experiences

What if managers and leaders at companies focused on a new goal: to elevate the human experience? Can we look at increasing the amount of humanity in the workplace by first measuring it and looking to enhance it? Measuring human experience is critical to a business's sustained growth. While it is important to measure how people feel about the company's product or service, it is equally important to measure an employee's experience at work.

Human emotion provides us with a framework for measuring human experience. A recent study found that when people are faced with a decision that can have both negative and positive outcomes, they are more likely to go with their emotional evaluation rather than their cognitive evaluation. For example, if you are tempted to buy ice cream, your mind is balancing the delight part of the experience (emotional) with the health aspect (cognitive). If the emotion that an employee feels towards the workplace is positive, they are likely to have a better experience.

Emotion is a dominant and fundamental factor in the decision-making process of humans. Understanding the human experience and the emotions driving it will allow organizations to measure and tailor their workplace experience, removing mismatches. The usual areas of mismatch in the workplace are the following: the work you do, the control you have over the work, the reward you get, the colleagues you work with, the fairness of the treatment you receive and the value system you are exposed to at work.

A mismatch in the work you do would mean that you either don't have the right skill or you are overloaded and have insufficient resources; a mismatch in control would mean that you don't have enough autonomy and have to constantly wait for approvals; a reward mismatch might mean that your work is not getting the recognition it deserves; a fairness mismatch might mean that for the same job, people are paid differently or someone is promoted out of term without clear reason. A value mismatch means that there are ethical, moral and legal conflicts in the workplace.

Human experience measurement can be done using a combination of surveys, focus group discussions and data analytics on various parameters like attrition, satisfaction, absenteeism, etc. There are multiple tools and techniques available, and you could choose to use a combination of them. By measuring your experience, you can then work towards improving it.

The End of the Average

The value of creating an average experience that suits all employees is diminishing. The US Air Force's search for the perfect fighter jet cockpit provides a valuable lesson. In the 1950s, air force engineers took on a huge project to measure the exact dimensions of an average man's body (only men were air force pilots in those days). From the length of the shin to the width between a fully extended thumb and little finger, no calculation was too small. Their goal was to design a seat and instruments that would be perfect for the average person. The glitch was that they discovered there were no people who were average on all measurements. They had built the perfect cockpit as per their measurement of the averages, but it fit no one. To their credit, they didn't give up and designed cockpits that were adjustable across the critical dimensions. That approach allowed people with all their distinct personal dimensions to create matches with their working environment.

This example shows us the importance of personalization. Just as in the case with designing jet fighters, there is no one-size-fits-all solution to designing the employee experience. Rather than trying to generate one ideal system, you should foster a flexible dialogue that can adjust to the needs of the workplace, the employee and the work. Companies should embrace the idea that developing their workplaces is a creative process. Fixing problems is an iterative process and could encompass the following:

Getting inputs from the users: While you often know what the issues are, you will always learn something new when you ask for input. The most direct route to identifying mismatches is to ask people (anonymously, if you wish) about their experiences at work and their suggestions for improvements. This starts a conversation with employees, and their responses generate ideas—some direct and some that need some thinking to fix. After gathering the input, it is essential to summarize the findings and share them publicly. A common complaint in workplaces is that, while surveys are a dime a dozen, feedback is rarely shared.

Look at various possible solutions: The next step is to work on solutions to the inputs received. You could look at a variety of creative problem-solving methods to arrive at solutions. It's good to test the solutions through rapid prototyping before shortlisting a few for a final discussion. You could even have a working group to present the final options to the larger community.

Get quick wins: Often, when designing solutions, it is more important to make small, tangible gains quickly rather than embark on a long journey towards a large gain. Quick wins showcase that progress is being made and more is on the way. You also need to communicate the win so that more people are willing to come forward and work on making the experience better for everyone.

Use human-centric principles for design: When redesigning experiences, simplify them wherever possible. Good design is all about simplicity, and by keeping things simple, you will arrive at a solution that is easier to implement. At this stage, the focus should be on the users of the enhanced experience.

Build in checkpoints so that changes can be made: Continuous assessment, adjustment and refinement are necessary for any developed innovations. Real progress always involves practice and course correction. Ongoing monitoring of the workplace experience through a process of change and continuous improvement can make the new design better.

Users and first-line managers are important pivot points for improving experiences because they are in the best position to identify problem areas and design better solutions. Given their trust and responsibility, they can help improve and customize the work experience for everyone.

* * *

Rather than discovering a silver bullet to improve experience, you need a fresh approach to thinking about human experience at work. The third decade of the twenty-first century calls for greater responsiveness to employee experiences, paying closer attention to their psychological motivations and greater flexibility in job design and work conditions. A better human experience at work helps bring out the best in the workers of the future. One of the things we should agree on is that employees who have a high experience score or believe their company is humane are much more likely to be motivated at work.

Chapter 6

Imagining Your Office of the Future

The best way to predict the future is to invent it.

—Alan Kay

Since the dawn of the industrial age, workers would visit a place of work and produce output as part of a collective endeavour. This was a change from the artisanal way of work that was the mainstay of small human habitations for centuries—the village blacksmith or tailor producing goods from his home establishment, which usually was a room below the dwelling occupied by his family. This shift was needed because, as the industrial revolution progressed, the tools of production became complex and expensive. It was not possible for a craftsman to invest in the machinery needed for production, and also to match the cost and quality of goods produced in factories. Gradually, what was produced by craftsmen in their home workshops was manufactured by industrial workers in a bigger place, like a factory. Eventually, the place of work changed for many people.

Factories needed administration, requiring additional people to support the working group. This led to the creation of the early office. In addition to machine operators and their supervisors, the factory now employed office workers to carry out various administrative tasks. Usually, the factory held some space for those who kept track of attendance and paid out wages. These offices were small and employed a few administrative staff who were very much part of the factory.

World War II was followed by an industrial boom, and the expansion of the factory brought the need for larger offices as formal management structures started increasing. The benefits of automation in manufacturing sparked ideas about how technology could similarly enable offices. The first signs of automation in the office started appearing with the introduction of tabulation machines, communication devices and other enablers for the office staff to be more efficient. Following the war, economic growth also led to the emergence of offices unconnected to factories. These businesses were into trading, finance, insurance and other activities that needed workers who mainly did desk jobs. Considering that people were used to the factory model, these offices also mirrored the factory as a place where people went and produced output. The 1960s saw a huge growth in non-factory-linked jobs, which necessitated large offices in cities and led to modern skyscrapers. The 1970s saw the construction of the World Trade Center in New York and other similar buildings. These office buildings were integrated with transport systems that enabled people to easily reach their offices. In fact, some of them had train stations in their basements. These transport systems were built to accommodate a large number of people commuting to work. The pattern of large-scale unidirectional commutes became familiar in most world cities as people left their homes for work and returned in the evening.

A large-scale transition from office-based, co-located work to remote work arguably began with some companies adopting work-from-home (WFH) policies in the 1970s, as soaring gasoline prices caused by the 1973 OAPEC oil embargo[1] made commuting more expensive. These policies were designed to allow employees to carry out some portions of their work at home or a nearby workspace with periodic visits to the office. This was welcomed by office workers as they were able to have better control over their time and perform errands such as school pick-ups, which were essential to balancing the needs of the dual-working family. While more offices and employees experimented with telecommuting and remote work as information technology improved, going to the office was still a necessary part of working life. The only exception was those rare people who could work as individual contributors removed from the office environment, like the artisans of old.

The Covid-19 pandemic forced workspaces to vacate in a short period of time. Tens of millions of people around the world suddenly shifted to a gigantic experiment of working from home, with homes suddenly functioning as offices using technology. The city centre and the transport system stood silent as people vacated their offices. The subsequent years saw a rise in remote work along with new tools for collaboration and working. The remote working experiment appeared more permanent than anyone had imagined. Some people even predicted the death of the office and the end of the city centre. But history shows that while sudden events can disturb or change the status quo, it takes effort and thought to make the change workable for all.

Have we come full circle in terms of our workplaces? From artisans working in their home workshops to factories of the industrial age to offices in city centres and then finally back to remote working in individual homes? It seems like we are now uniquely placed to imagine the ideal workspace of the future. Digitization and networking are increasingly becoming part of our regular workday. Today's business environment needs to allow for flexibility in terms of work, but it also needs to consider the need for social connections and the benefits of working in a common place. In this chapter, we will examine two areas—the workplace of the future and how one thrives and manages in this new world of work.

Technology and the Office

When we look at workplace technology, its evolution has been surprisingly rapid over the past decade. Workplace technology, whether its computing devices, broadband speeds, connectivity, cloud computing, video conferencing, AI systems or virtual reality technology—all of this improved exponentially. At the same time, the cost of technology has shrunk to the extent that even a very small business can have facilities that were only available in large offices a few years ago. A major result of this is that practically every work-related action can be performed from the comfort of one's phone. In effect, we can say that the office is now travelling with the worker instead of the worker commuting to the office.

Another major aspect of change is the work location. Our cities are getting transformed into megacities with increased migration of labour as well as expansion into suburbia. It will no longer be feasible for employees to follow the unidirectional commute patterns of the past. Our cities will soon evolve into a collection of integrated living, working and community spaces. Imagine a group of buildings in the city block where a set of floors is reserved for residences, another set for offices and a third set for a hotel, with some floors reserved for common amenities, schools, recreational spaces and so on. People will employ a pay-as-you-use model of living and prefer to live where they can balance their work and personal needs. Most people will see an improvement in their work–life balance as the commute will be within a city block, there will be no need for cars and every facility for quality living will be within easy access.

Connecting the benefits of the evolution of office technologies and changes in the design of habitation spaces will offer us a new perspective on the future way of working. Let's look at how.

In a few years, the collaboration technology available for work would have gotten markedly better. This will allow us to work in a mixed-reality environment. For instance, imagine that you are working remotely. You will be able to open the collaboration software and see your entire team, just as you would if you were in an actual office using virtual reality. You could click on a particular colleague's image and speak to them over video in the same manner as you would have walked across and spoken to them if both of you were in the office. If you needed to meet with your whole team, you would be able to get into a virtual meeting room for a quick whiteboarding exercise. Advancements in virtual reality technology and the capabilities of collaboration software to operate multi-channel feeds will seamlessly blend remote work with physical work.

Now let's look at the design of the office itself. For a long time, the office was designed around a central core with utilities such as elevators, cabling and bathrooms.

The floor was designed to accommodate network and power cables. Once laid and connected, the workstations were placed in a way that could accommodate the network, telephones and power points. This is why most offices looked almost identical, except for the wallpaper. These offices were designed to maximize the use of electrical and network points, rather than considering the needs of humans and their work.

Can we now redesign the office to make it useful for humans? With new wireless and cloud technology, you don't need any network or power points around cubicles. Also, most people will not come into the office every day and will not need permanent workspaces. The office can be redesigned to better accommodate human needs. People will come to the office for a combination of reasons—personal connection, collaborative work or solitary focus time. The office should seamlessly provide for all three purposes by incorporating spaces that allow for different needs and using technology to allocate these spaces to individuals based on their needs. Instead of being centred on a core office and cubicles, the office will be a collection of zones, such as collaboration areas, individual quiet areas, spaces that allow for serendipitous meetings like atriums, cafeterias, gardens, etc.

The emotion a modern office needs to convey to its occupants is that you belong and have a place that you can use for your work needs, either to focus effort, host someone or interact with your team in a productive way. The attention given to the aspects of design, facilities and quality of the experience go on to convey the fact that you matter and that your happiness and productivity are important.

One universal truth is that you cannot get people to deliver world-class output with poor technology and bad office surroundings. While we have examples of great companies being founded in garages, we do not have any examples of successful companies that have managed to succeed long-term without investments in technology and good office infrastructure. Both should be functional, comfortable and designed with the user in mind. Over the past few years, we have seen futuristic office designs from many companies, including Apple, that focus on human-centric design incorporating collaboration, innovation, technology and wellness.

Work Design and the Office

Go to any modern office, and the cubicle or partitioned workspaces will be the default pattern for most of them. Sometimes the office resembles a maze, both literally and metaphorically. This kind of design probably served its purpose when organizations operated in functional silos and were hierarchical. Today, the nature of work and the use of the office have considerably changed. The modern office needs to be designed around the work being performed. For example, an architectural firm doesn't function in the same way as an insurance company. Their offices must be designed differently.

Let's say that a software development team has decided to work out of a physical office for the next two weeks to complete an important project that needs close collaboration. The office enablement technology must direct the team members to a space that is optimized for their project needs. Since their visit requires a high amount of collaboration with other team members on the project, everyone who is associated with the activity is routed to a particular area that is designed for this purpose.

Workspaces will be pre-assigned to them, which will be digitally customized to their needs. The seating layout would be determined by analysing the project's workflow and designing seating based on the amount of interaction needed between team members. The office software will do this seamlessly, requiring no effort from the employee's end. The reduced time and increased productivity will make the experience of working out of the physical office seem almost magical.

During the time the team works out of the physical office, the office enablement software could schedule a set of individual meetings for team members with relevant departments. It could even schedule routine maintenance slots with IT for their laptops. Technology can also enable each participant to receive real-time information on how the day is progressing in terms of the accomplishment of project goals, provide course corrections and even plan the next day at the office in the same way.

The above is not a futuristic scenario. All that is described above is possible using today's technology. For example, companies can access project status as well as user data using their enterprise management software. This gives them a good understanding of individual and teamwork habits, their networks, their work status and their collaboration needs. Using an AI-based tool, the software will then help plan optimum usage for office work and guide the team to be more productive in the office.

Another way technology can help reduce barriers to collaboration is to optimize usage of office networks. You could either have a wayfinding algorithm to locate colleagues and fix meeting spaces or you could chart a path for an optimum walk that will connect you to colleagues who could help you solve the problem at hand. For example, if you were assigned a cost optimization project to complete, AI-based software could examine your project plan, past meeting schedules and team composition. The software would then superimpose this data with the existing organizational data and work out an optimal schedule for your day at the office. The software would match you to people with relevant skillsets for your needs, identify their availability, fix meeting slots and even prepare a summary note about the purpose of the meeting so that the meeting is productive. Post-meeting, you will both receive a summary of the discussion and your virtual assistant will schedule any follow ups needed.

Survey tools will allow managers and HR to quickly check in with employees on their concerns on a single day and work out solutions in a real-time manner. For example, if there is a concern about delayed suburban rail services, employees could get a real-time feed on the optimal time to leave the office and the software could then adjust meeting times accordingly. Using such interventions, companies could course correct and proactively address issues that impact morale, all adding to the dimension of care through intelligent usage of data and technology.

Future office workers can enjoy greater flexibility thanks to the combination of technology and better work design. It allows them to plan their work and life so that they can be more productive, as well as balance their personal commitments. The most important aspect is that the combination of technological interventions and work design enables people to seamlessly integrate remote workers with teams who are present at the office.

How Does One Thrive in the New World of Work?

From the era when individual artisans produced goods in their home workshops to more recent times where people were typing away at their keyboards to perform various tasks, the change an average worker could expect to see in the way they performed their job was minimal. For example, a typist could see themselves gainfully employed throughout their work life, using the typewriter for communication. Today, you would be lucky if the office application you use stays the same the next year—think of Slack, Google Hangouts, Yammer, etc. Now, from the time someone joins their profession to the time they leave, the pace of change in technology has everyone scrambling to keep up. Staying up-to-date with technology is more than just experimenting with emerging technologies like AI or dealing with new software. It's about getting the most out of the available technological tools so that you are productive and ahead of the curve in terms of readiness. The faster you step up to learn and embrace change, the better your chances of success in the workplace of the future.

Here are a few thoughts that can help us thrive in the evolving world of work.

1. **Technology improves productivity:** New technologies in the workplace will free up time and enable you to focus on more challenging, interesting and impactful projects. Your goal is to see how each new available tool can improve your productivity by experimenting with it.
2. **Train to use the new technology:** Whenever a new technology is introduced, substantial investments are put into training people. Typically, both the technology provider as well as the company investing in it will provide training for users. Don't miss out on this opportunity and avail of the training being offered.

3. **Learn from early adapters:** There will always be early adapters for any new technology. It's a good idea to reach out to these early birds and work along with them to learn and improve your skills.
4. **Help others learn:** Teaching someone a new technology doubles your own learning. Also, sometimes technology can also cause stress in people. See if you can help people out. And they will reciprocate by providing assistance when needed.

Many of us still underestimate the power of technological change. Just think of all the things you can do with your smart phone now that you couldn't do before. While it's good to notice how much the phone has improved, think of the time it took you to start using some of its features. You could have started using these features earlier and benefited from them. The same goes for any other office technology.

Working with Virtual Assistants

As humans, we have multiple interests and there are many things that we would like to do. The limitation to accomplishing all that we would like to do is that we must simultaneously deal with the routine and the mundane in our lives. This takes us away from spending our time creating something, learning or just dreaming. Till now, only those senior in the work hierarchy could afford themselves an assistant who could take away the burden of routine activities and allow them to focus.

Today, we can all have a virtual assistant. They could either be standalone ones like Amazon's Alexa or be embedded in your office suite like Microsoft Copilot.

Over the next few years, we will be able to change the way we work thanks to the evolution of these virtual assistants. These assistants combine large language models with your cloud data to improve your productivity. Even in a nascent state, they represent a step change in the way we interact with machines. Since they function using our spoken language, they can work the same way as human assistants.

For example, Microsoft Copilot is integrated with the applications you use daily and works alongside them. You could be speaking to your virtual assistant and instructing it, for example, 'prepare a presentation based on the meeting we had to discuss the new product launch' or 'send a feedback mail to Sam based on the discussion we had about her performance'. Of course, as a user, you are still in control with regards to the final output, but as these assistants evolve, requests such as 'book me a ticket to Delhi on Wednesday morning' will be fairly automatic in terms of checking your calendar for scheduling the time, your past flight preferences, availability of seats on the airline system and many other things that you would spend time figuring out, will be done automatically and only a final approval will be needed to proceed.

So how does one work with virtual assistants? The first thing you should aim for is to use them to jump-start your work. For example, you could ask your assistant to give you the first draft of a document you need to produce. By doing this, it will save you the time you normally spend sourcing the material, putting it in order, editing and so on. You can then focus on putting your unique ideas into the document. Similarly, it could produce a basic presentation or analyse data and give you useful graphs that you could develop further. We all want to focus on the 20 per cent of our work that really matters, but 80 per cent of our time is consumed with busywork that bogs us down. Having a virtual assistant like Copilot lightens the load.[2] Let's take email as an example. A trained virtual assistant could quickly help you clear your inbox by following some simple rules. In a meeting, it could summarize key discussion points, including individual opinions and give everyone attending the meeting a set of action items.

The progress of virtual assistants is not limited to booking tickets or doing pre-work for a presentation. GitHub, the world's largest AI-powered developer platform, helps unlock productivity and a better experience for developers. It shoulders the boring and repetitive tasks of writing code and makes room for developers to enjoy more meaningful work that involves critical thinking and problem solving. It makes software developers more productive and helps them save time they would otherwise spend on getting the basics in place, searching for information or coding algorithms. As technology evolves, there will be other similar assistants available to make you more productive.

Every company and individual have a massive reservoir of data and insights in the enterprise system that are largely inaccessible and untapped. What these assistants do is seamlessly work across your data that resides on multiple devices and apps. They then get you the real-time information you need to accomplish a task. Since they are designed to constantly learn, they will improve the more you use them. These virtual assistants will fundamentally change how people work with AI and how AI works with people. Your focus should be to get ahead of the learning curve. If you can first embrace the power of office assistants and use them regularly, you will gain an advantage at your workplace.

Towards a Better Workplace

It is estimated that a typical office worker takes about two million breaths in the office in a year.[3] Well, even if the number is an estimate, it's something to think about the role our office surroundings play in our health and well-being. Among the many things we learnt during the recent pandemic, one of them was the need to invest in healthier workspaces in terms of air quality, working environment and avenues for enhanced wellness. Offices play a major role in the spread of disease among the working population, but if designed and operated smartly, they can also improve our health.

Given the global shortage of talent, companies are eager to find new ways to attract and retain people. One of the retention levers is investment in better workspaces. Let's look at the key elements that make up a healthy workspace: ventilation and air quality; temperature; moisture; dust; pests and allergens; safety and security; water quality; noise levels; lighting and outside vistas. All these parameters are important and an improvement in them will increase productivity, while a reversal will decrease it.

One of the most common complaints is the office temperature. Some people find it too high and others too low. We conducted an experiment in an office that I worked in. By installing a very simple thermostat and airflow control, we improved employee comfort levels. This system allowed the air conditioning system to go off in cooling mode if the ambient temperature outside was at a comfortable level. The air circulation system then allowed only fresh air to flow indoors. We also allowed multiple small blowers for users to control airflow in the areas where they were sitting, in place of the large common blower. Interestingly, the system paid for itself as it consumed less energy.

Let's look at an interesting concept called biophilic design. In simple terms it means that you design the office in a way that increases the connectivity building occupants have with nature. This approach incorporates various natural elements into the design. The idea is not new and city planners have used it since time immemorial, the oldest example being the Hanging Gardens of Babylon. We depend on nature for survival and fulfillment. Creating an office that gives its occupants a better connection with nature is simple and just requires the right focus and intelligent design.

Investing in office automation technology is another aspect of building a better workspace. Software that monitors building systems has several advantages. It can perform real-time tests on parameters such as temperature, air quality, etc. and make adjustments to various equipment like lighting and air conditioning for optimal usage, thereby making the office space both environmentally friendly and saving money at the same time. Inhabitants of large cities frequently experience poor air quality. If you can provide filtration and a clean air system, they would then have access to clean air for a good part of their day, thereby increasing their quality of life.[4]

Costs are a critical factor in office systems. With better collaboration technologies, modern offices already provide substantial savings in terms of consumables, such as paper and printing ink. The use of tablets and digital whiteboards will increase, enhancing collaboration and efficiency in sharing and retrieving documents. Sensors, such as smart lighting or HVAC (heating, ventilation, air conditioning) systems, will reduce costs as they turn on when triggered by presence detection or various environmental stimuli.[5]

One of the challenges will be to reconfigure and optimize the workplace to match real-time data. By doing this, you can measure what is successful and what can be improved. As an organization, it's good practice to track the key performance parameters required for a healthy office. We can call these the office health KPIs (key performance indicators). Health drives productivity and performance, and these are important parameters to track. You need to track office performance as well as that of the people inhabiting it. These need to be communicated to the people using the building—it shows care as well as provides transparency.

The Most-Used Office Space

We spend a lot of time at work, and unless you are one of those hermits who eats at your desk, it's likely you will spend a fair bit of that time in the office cafeteria. We cannot have a healthy workplace strategy without considering the cafeteria.

The office cafeteria is a good starting point for encouraging health, nutrition and wellness among employees. The cafeteria should ideally be an open, airy space with a lot of natural light and great views. I recently visited an office whose entry point is through the cafeteria. You could grab some coffee or a snack as you enter, and even conduct your work meetings. You could then take an elevator or a ramp to other parts of the office as per your needs, but the entrance is a great way to welcome you into the workplace. A true example of reaching the heart through the stomach.

Since the office cafeteria is where people come to relax and refuel, it is a great place to promote healthy eating practices. Some workplaces promote fruit and vegetables more openly than sodas or snacks. They are prominently displayed at the very start of the food service line, encouraging employees to opt for these healthier options. Some companies stock a lot of herbal teas, milk, fruit and nuts to encourage healthy snacking throughout the day. You can encourage your employees, as well as food vendors, to actively participate.

Apart from meals, the cafeteria is also where people gather to enjoy casual social interactions. Good design can encourage and enable such interactions in a safe, organic way. Some companies design dual-use spaces that can accommodate large employee or client events.

The Future of Office Technology

Workplace technology is on an exponential development curve. However, human imagination is needed to make this work synchronously to aid productivity instead of adding to the burden. For instance, effective online collaboration tools will require a redesign of the way people work in the physical office. Otherwise, there is no reason why they should come to the office to collaborate, as they could do so online. We must use what is best for the purpose we have in mind, whether it's the latest technology or something that people have used for a while. The purpose is what should drive the decision.

The key technologies that will make a difference in the modern workplace are:

- **Messaging technology:** Team members must constantly interact with each other to accomplish their work, and this interaction must happen regardless of where they are located. So, offices will need to have real-time messaging technology that shows when a team member is available for immediate collaboration. The same messaging technology should also handle asynchronous collaboration when real-time is not needed, so the focus time of colleagues can be optimized. For example, a queuing and prioritizing system will work great in the messaging system to allow for asynchronous work.

- **Workflows and people flows:** Technology has enabled a better flow of work as well as people. While workflow refers to the movement of work (like documents) through a sequence of tasks that are related to a business process. The term 'people flow' refers to the movement of individuals within a process. For example, someone might prefer a quiet place to work or need a space for collaboration. The office space needs to be planned for people's movement to suit occupants as they perform different tasks during the day. This increases productivity through a reduction of wasted effort that went into back-and-forth communication and moments. Office planning platforms like Integrated Workplace Management System (IWMS) help you to plan workflow quickly and reduce inefficiencies. Thanks to available systems, it no longer takes days or weeks to repurpose a workspace or change the dynamics of an office. With better workflow designs, facility managers can adapt the workplace in minutes to shave hours or days off project timelines and tasks.
- **Broad asset accessibility:** The enterprise cloud is arguably the most influential workplace

technology of the last two decades. Think about what the cloud offers—broad access to any digital assets, anytime, anywhere. This level of accessibility has become so ingrained in what we do that we often take it for granted. As much as the business cloud has changed the traditional workplace, it's also the biggest catalyst for working remotely. In fact, this technology is growing more powerful every day through innovations in edge computing and decentralized server networks. More importantly, the availability of data allows analytics and AI systems to work in the backend to provide insights and solutions that otherwise would not have been possible.

Finally, we need to ask: How does technology affect productivity? If it's not evident already, technology has been the most significant stimulus for improving employee productivity and efficiency. Try doing your job without computers, email, messaging apps, cloud storage or the ability to reserve a workspace, contribute to a shared document or even connect with colleagues around the world. It's likely impossible to work without technology in today's climate. Even if you could manage it, you'd be light years behind. Technology touches every aspect of work—how, where and even when we accomplish it. The result of ever-increasing advancements in technological tools is evident in everything, from how we communicate to the scope of our daily work. Thanks to workplace technologies, we're ever-moving, constantly communicating and consistently accomplishing, no matter where or what we're doing.

Let's look at some examples of what different companies are doing with technology and how they are making a difference in their workforce.

Company A: operates large retail stores. It has implemented an AI-based employee scheduling system to optimize schedules based on employee availability, workload and store traffic.

Company B: has implemented a data-driven HR system using analytics and machine learning to identify factors contributing to employee turnover and engagement. It develops targeted strategies and interventions to improve employee retention and satisfaction.

Company C: has implemented a wellness programme that uses wearable technology to track employees' physical activity and health metrics. It provides personalized coaching and support to help employees improve their health and well-being.

Company D: uses a career development platform designed in-house. It provides employees with personalized learning and development opportunities, career pathing and job matching tools to help them navigate their career paths within the company.

A Thriving Future Workplace

So, how does one thrive in the new workplace? Today we have a great opportunity to adapt to the changes, let go of our old ways of working, quickly learn new things and improve our ability to impact the business. Here are some things to keep in mind:

You are more empowered: From going to an office every morning, we have now changed the way we see work fitting into our lives. The future workplace is going to be one that will face shortages of both skills and talent. So, anyone with a skill set that's in demand will be empowered. You could design the way you work and your workplace to suit your needs.

Work is the key, not management: The shift is in looking at the work delivered and not in managing people. The manager's role will largely be to enable people to give their best and not get people to work for you.

Peers are collaborators: People will no longer be pitted against one another to measure and reward performance. Teams will have complementary but exclusive skill sets. The culture of the team will need to be such that peers are seen as collaborators who will help us achieve more together.

Intrinsic motivation: You should not tie your learning and adaptability to outdated rewards and threats. You need to tap into your intrinsic motivation and connect your drivers to larger business objectives.

We're recognizing that some work can be done anywhere. But there is some work, such as coaching, mentoring and creative interactions, that does require people to be together regularly. With the advent of technology, employees will be able to better plan their schedules accordingly.

Each of us will drive the future of work. From pushing towards new trends such as BYOD (bring your own device) in the office to launching innovative social media campaigns and adopting collaborative tools such as Dropbox, Skype, Slack and Zoom, we all play a role in this change. The boundary between using technology for our personal use and bringing it into the office is porous, and it shows that the future office will be fun, innovative and centred on human connections. The purpose of a workspace has not changed from the time the craftsman used their skills to earn a living and produce things of value to the people around them. Tools, technologies, the way of working and the place of work might have all evolved, but as long as we don't forget our purpose, we are on the right track.

Chapter 7

Failing Successfully

There is only one thing that makes a dream impossible to achieve: the fear of failure.

—Paulo Coelho, *The Alchemist*

On most days, the line to get into the Smithsonian Air and Space Museum in Washington DC stretches around a couple of blocks from the entrance on Independence Avenue. The Wright Flyer is one of the first displays you will see once you get inside. The Wright Flyer deserves its place because of its significance in letting humans take flight. The Wright Flyer made the first sustained flight by a manned, heavier-than-air, powered and controlled aircraft on 17 December 1903. Invented and flown by brothers Orville and Wilbur Wright, it marked the beginning of modern aviation.

The flyer on display at the museum is the original machine that made the first human flight over 100 years ago on a remote beach in North Carolina, except for the canvas on the wings that needed replacement. It took them four years of experimentation in their bicycle workshop to get everything right. After building and testing three full-sized gliders, the Wright brothers' first powered airplane flew at Kitty Hawk, North Carolina, on 17 December 1903, making a twelve-second flight, travelling 36 m (120 ft), with Orville piloting. The best flight of the day, with Wilbur at the controls, covered 255.6 m (852 ft) in fifty-nine seconds.

Today, when we see the 500-tonne Airbus 380s flying 500-odd passengers across the Atlantic, we don't realize that many of the inventions of the Wright brothers survive to this day in modern aircraft, such as the aerofoil canvas wing, which they perfected in air tunnels after observing bird wings, the dual engine, the flaps to control lift, etc. These innovations are still used today, with some modifications.

What stands out about the Wright brothers' pursuit of flight is the number of detailed designs and experiments conducted on every aspect of the design. Their attention to detail and meticulous note-taking are admirable. Even more significant was their treatment of every experiment as a learning exercise, particularly the ones that did not succeed. The causes of failure were captured in detail, and modifications were made to the design so that the next trial would yield better or different results. Success came through their failed experiments.

Moreover, the process that the Wright brothers used to analyse a problem and experiment with a solution based on an idea from another application helped them reach their goal. For example, they realized that a successful flyer would require wings to generate lift, a propulsion system to move it through the air and a system to control the craft in flight. The brothers were professional bicycle mechanics, so many of their designs emerged from the principles of riding a bicycle—the control is in the hands of the user and the balance of the human on the machine is crucial. They used the same principle for their flying machine.

Instead of controlling the machine by shifting the weight of the pilot, as in a bicycle, they devised a mechanism to control the plane by shifting the wings. They experimented with various mechanical controls before arriving at a helical twist across the wings that could increase or decrease the lift on either side. Such controls, powered by hydraulic and electronic systems, are used in the wings of modern aircraft even today.

They even experimented with different locations until they arrived at the right place for their first flight. Realizing that their hometown Dayton had low winds and flat terrain, they studied the weather statistics of nearby areas before choosing Kitty Hawk, which offered moderate winds, had sand dunes for the height needed for the launch and plenty of soft sand for landing.

Many of the early experiments the brothers undertook were on gliders. They solved various problems like lift, control, weight, wing design, etc. before putting a human on the machine. The early gliders were quite disappointing in terms of results, as the problem of lift and control was difficult to resolve.

The Wright brothers even constructed a small wind tunnel to gather their own information on the behaviour of various wing designs when exposed to a wind stream. They preferred to obtain their own data instead of relying on others. During the fall and early winter of 1901, the Wrights tested between 100 and 200 designs in their wind tunnel.

What the Wright brothers' experimental approach shows is that there is rarely success without failure. As you rise in your career, you are going to fail many times. The same happens to entrepreneurs when they start companies or even to established companies as they venture into new areas. Many notable success stories are the result of numerous failures. Henry Ford went bankrupt before starting the Ford Motor Company; Thomas Edison and his colleagues tested thousands of materials before creating the carbon filament light bulb and Abraham Lincoln failed[1] many times before being elected President in 1860. It's said that failure doesn't stop a person; it's how you handle the failure that can stop you. While discussing his various failed experiments, Thomas Edison's associate once said to him, 'Isn't it a shame that with the tremendous amount of work you have done, you haven't been able to get any results?' Edison replied, 'Results! Why, man, I have gotten a lot of results! I know several thousand things that won't work.' In his lifetime, Thomas Edison earned 1093 US patents.

Most of us enter the corporate world after a graduate or post-graduate degree. The academic world provides a clearer path to success by allowing for controlled failure through tests and assignments, with opportunities to learn from the failure. For example, an exam helps you find out how much you have learnt in class. You get opportunities to do the exam again if your first attempt did not work out. Once you clear the exams, you move to a higher class. Rarely in the corporate world do you find the path so unobstructed or success so easily defined. As you pursue your career goals, you are going to fail on some occasions or, more importantly, not achieve what you define as success. When that happens, how you handle failure is very important.

One of the most frequently asked questions when I meet people in their early careers is about growth. Often, there is angst about missing out on an obvious growth step in one's career through a promotion, a visible change in designation or role. The focus is less about learning from the perceived failure and more about somehow attaining the milestone. The Wright brothers focused on learning and making changes to their approach. They didn't simply focus on flying. Einstein once made a comment about going ahead without learning. He said that if you repeat the same experiment a second time, what makes you think that it will give you different results?

At its most basic definition, failure is the lack of success. It can take on many shapes and forms. Failure could mean you were unable to get the promotion you anticipated, failed to land a big sale or found yourself in the wrong job. The only constant about failures is their abundance. As you progress in your career, you're going to fail, so it's a good idea to build failure into your plan, not by being pessimistic but by treating it as a learning opportunity.

There are two important aspects to consider during your journey:

i. Your definition of success
ii. Learning from the failures

Both are equally important. Remember, it's not failure; it's how you handle failure that defines your future success. Let's look at the definition of failure as well as how to learn from it.

Defining Your Success

To quote the nineteenth-century essayist, Ralph Waldo Emerson, success is: 'To laugh often and much; to win the respect of intelligent people and the affection of children . . . to appreciate the beauty; to find the best in others; to leave the world a bit better, whether by a healthy child or a garden patch . . . to know even one life has breathed easier because you have lived. This is to have succeeded.'[2]

While Emerson might be abstract in his definition, in the corporate world, success is being happy with your job, what you do every day at work, whether you get up every morning with the eagerness to get to work, whether you enjoy working with colleagues and whether your workplace treats you fairly with appreciation for a job well done.

The definition of success needs to be absolute for you, not measured relative to others. The comparison highway is the biggest source of unhappiness in companies. We set benchmarks for comparing ourselves to others. For example, you may feel you are lagging in terms of a designation, are at a lower compensation level or even that the room where you sit is smaller.

As a publicly listed company, it was mandatory for my workplace to publish the annual salaries of key executives earning above a threshold. This was part of our financial reporting and was done once a year. The minute the upload was done and information was publicly available, a few people would approach their managers or human resources with questions about why they were paid lower than someone else who seemed to be at their benchmark. It's pertinent to note that the names listed in this report were people who had reached the pinnacle of their careers. On an absolute basis, they would be a very small percentage of the company's workforce and would be earning a salary much higher than the average of the organization. But some employees would get upset and treat this as a personal failure.

Hence, it's important to define what success means for you. Take a few minutes to do the following exercise:

For every five years of your career span, write down what you would define as success for you, whether it's reaching a particular position, a salary level, a qualification and so on. You could do this for two cycles of five years each, so that at any point in time, you have a definition of success laid out for the next ten years. Ideally, you should ignore anything beyond what you have written. If you need to change anything in the first five-year cycle, you should do so only if it's extremely important. You could make changes to the second five-year cycle. As you progress in your career, your goals for success will mature.

Your goals should be realistic and meaningful for you. You should keep this sheet private and not share it with anyone else. Be sure to save the sheet so that you can refer to it whenever you need it.

	0–5 years	5–10 years
Career	• Be recognized as among the top 10 per cent performers in the company • Get selected for an assignment in another country	• Promoted to general manager of a business division • Compensation of 'x' amount
Personal	• Complete a hike to the base camp of Mt Everest. • Start a regular savings plan • Buy a car	• Invest in a house • Run a half marathon
Learning	• Learn spoken German • Speak at a TEDx conference on a subject	• Do a part time executive education programme in business management

Once you've identified your areas of success, do not be swayed by others. Be wary of the projected success that comes from the social media posts of other people because they seldom show their failures online. You are successful when you have achieved what you set out to do.

Learning from Failure

The second part of the journey is learning from every failure. The reason for a particular failure could be that you did not have full information or did not anticipate the challenges of a particular task well. It could also be that the reasons are beyond your control. Either way, you need to take time to organize your thoughts after a failure and categorize them into what you could have done better. The question to ask of yourself is: if I were to do this task again, how would I do it differently?

What happens to all of us after a failure is that we tend to feel bad about it. Remember what the Wright brothers did? They expected failure to happen and after every experiment, they went back and made detailed notes about their learning. Similarly, if we change our view to make every failure a learning opportunity, we will have a lot of work to do. You will have a detailed analysis of what went wrong, a list of changes you will make to the approach, a new idea you might want to try out and so on.[3]

Let's take the example of a commonly faced situation in companies. People change their jobs and companies regularly. Some of these career changes do not work out and are considered failures. Rarely does either the hiring company or the employee pause to do a detailed analysis of why the failure happened. No one learns from this failure, treating it as a poor decision. After an unplanned exit, the individual goes through a period of uncertainty, sometimes accompanied by stress or depression and then proceeds to join another place. The company will then hire another person with a similar approach. It's quite likely that all three entities—the employee and both companies—will benefit from doing a detailed analysis of the failure—the causes behind why the employment did not work out and what can be done to correct it the next time.

There are three stakeholders here: the employee, the company that he or she left and the new hiring company. For example, consider a failure analysis like the one below:

	Causes	**Fixes**
Individual Employee	• Did not have the required skills to perform the role. • Working with the team—as a first-time manager, found it difficult to lead a team.	• Carefully evaluate skills needed for the role and work out a ninety-day plan for upskilling if needed. • Improve team handling and resourcing skills.
Exiting Company	• Integration issues and feedback from customers was not positive. • Team complaints about leadership style.	• Detailed onboarding programme with regular customer feedback. • Manager assessment and development plan.

Hiring Company	• Analyse in detail reasons for leaving prior company. • Assessment centre for candidate evaluation.	• Adequate reference checks including informal ones. • A settling in plan based on inputs from the assessment. • A 360-degree feedback after six months of joining.

You can conduct a failure analysis for any situation. It does not take much time and the learning is immense. It's important to be honest, as this is a learning exercise for everyone involved.

Years ago, I was part of a group of students constructing a low-cost pick-and-place robot for our project submission during our undergraduate studies in engineering. This robot did not come out the way we had thought it would. We went wrong in many places, and it took several days and nights just before the submission deadline to make the robot work. In fact, the robot started working just a few minutes before the project evaluation. To give you an example of failure analysis, I have used this robot as an object of interest.

The definition of success: What a robot should look like varies among people, depending on which movie they have in mind. Each team member had a different view of what the robot should be like. For the project to be termed a success (success definition), the cost had to be reasonable, and the robot needed to pick up an object, place it in a desired position and be built.

Iterative design process: We expected our prototype to be the final design. Any design process, be it mechanical or paper-based, needs several tries to get right. Each stage requires tweaking of the original plan to shape the concept into reality. If the team had done several prototypes, even using cardboard models, the design flaws would have shown up earlier instead of a few hours before the deadline.

Project plan: We had more than six months to make the robot, yet we ran out of time. Having a project plan and working towards milestones would have ensured timely execution. The last few days could have been spent testing out the prototype in different conditions.

Teamwork: Not everyone in the team had uniform expertise, but with some thought, we could have planned team resources better and each one could have contributed using their strengths.

I have just used a college project to give you an example of how to do a failure analysis. The number of areas to analyse will increase in a complex project, but the process is the same. You write down all the areas that did not work and explain why. Once you have done this, do it differently on your next attempt.

Making Moon Shots Work

In July 2023, the Indian Space Research Organisation (ISRO) launched a mission to attempt a soft landing on the surface of the moon. This mission was launched four years after their first attempt crash-landed on the surface of the moon. This time, the mission was flawless, resulting in a perfect soft landing on the South Pole of the moon, a place where no other country had landed anything before. In the intervening four years, ISRO implemented several improvements to the mission after a detailed failure analysis of the first mission.

There are four important phases before a lander can touch down on the moon: the rough braking phase, the altitude hold phase, the fine braking phase and the landing phase. ISRO's analysis showed that in the previous attempt with Chandrayaan-2, the rough braking phase was executed perfectly. Problems started when the lander received twice the necessary thrust. The guidance system was unable to handle this massive difference in thrust and malfunctioned. Moreover, the control system in the fine braking phase could not correct the error of the earlier phase, which resulted in the lander crashing on the surface of the moon.

Ahead of the launch, ISRO spoke about an interesting design concept they had adopted. They termed it 'failure-based design' wherein they had designed for the rover to land successfully on the moon even if some things didn't go as per plan. Whether you are trying to land on the moon or submit your school project, the iterations in design take the same path. Some of the changes ISRO put in place for the Chandrayaan-3 mission included stronger legs for the lander to take higher velocities, solar panels on additional surfaces in case it landed at a different angle or plane, two engines instead of one, adding more fuel so that it could handle a deviation and so on. While the new lander was about 250 kg heavier, it was substantially more robust to handle failure.

Launched on 14 July 2023, Chandrayaan-3 entered the lunar orbit on 5 August and touched down on the lunar south pole region on 23 August, making India the fourth country to successfully land on the moon and the first to do so near the lunar south pole. ISRO learnt from failure and built it into success the second time. If the second attempt failed, they were ready for a third attempt with more changes.

Having a Growth Mindset

Over thirty years ago, Prof. Carol Dweck and her colleagues at Stanford began researching student's attitudes towards failure and learning. Their research found that the way students handled failure varied widely. Some students rebounded after a large failure, but many others were upset even with the slightest setbacks. They found that the mindsets of these two groups of students were different. They termed these 'fixed mindset' and 'growth mindset'. This categorization was based on the underlying beliefs people have about their intelligence and how they approach a learning situation. The students with a growth mindset believed that they could get smarter through their efforts. Naturally, they put in more time and effort into learning.

Further research in neuroscience[4] by the National Institute of Health reinforces the linkages between mindsets and achievement. The findings tell us that our brain is malleable. If our experiences are wider, the networks in our brain develop further, either through new pathways or by strengthening existing ones. More interestingly, the research shows that we can improve our neural growth based on the actions we take—learning more, allowing failure, trying new things, meeting new people and so on. If you believe your brain can grow, you tend to behave differently and acquire a growth mindset.

What are the consequences of believing that your intelligence or personality is malleable rather than fixed? I have encountered many people who seem to have one super arching goal, which is to succeed—at work, at university, in their career marks or in personal relationships. They tend to avoid taking risks that might end in failure, thereby letting go of many potential opportunities. Then there are others who are willing to experiment, to fail and to learn.

Let's explore how we can change our approach to incorporate failure into our path to success.

1. **What you start with:** Just like a hand dealt in a game of cards, you start with a set of traits and privileges influenced by your personality, home environment, etc. View them as just a starting point for development. With these basic qualities, you can achieve whatever you want through your efforts. You would be familiar with stories about someone starting from a privileged background but not achieving anything or about someone who came from an adverse situation and achieved remarkable success. What happens to you depends largely on what you do with the things you start with.
2. **Passion for learning:** No matter where you are, you can get better. Look for work assignments that stretch you. Similarly, spend more time with managers who will challenge you to grow. The passion for stretching yourself and persisting along the path is a hallmark of the growth mindset. Warren Buffet and his friend, the late Charlie Munger, who co-founded the world's most profitable firm, Berkshire Hathaway, claimed to spend most of their time reading up on different subjects and thinking. They believed learning helped them make better decisions. Their goal, in their own words, was to learn something new every day.
3. **Tolerate ambiguity and stress:** Maximum learning happens during challenging times. Muscles build when they are put under maximum stress and the same is true for your brain. A difficult work assignment, travelling to an unfamiliar location,

etc. builds up your capability, which you can use to be helpful in future situations.

4. **What others think doesn't matter:** Every situation doesn't need confirmation that you are on the right path, have the right intelligence and so on. Stop evaluating every situation with questions like, Will I succeed or fail? Will I be accepted or rejected? Will I be seen as a winner or a loser? People have short memories, and you can move on.
5. **Don't assign blame for failure:** Learning comes with risks. I'm not referring to big risks, but everyday decisions to do something that seems a little difficult. When you take on a growth mindset, failure is something to be faced, dealt with and learned from. It doesn't make it a less painful experience. Basketball coach John Wooden tells his players that you are not a failure until you start to assign blame. Once you do that, then you stop learning from your mistakes and begin to deny them.

People usually take one of two approaches when faced with a problem. They either see it as a challenge that stretches them too thin but consider themselves smart enough to solve it. The other approach is to wait for others to solve the problem. In the first approach, you assume ownership of the problem and learn from working towards a solution. In the second case, you don't.

Design Thinking

In the IT services industry, when a project fails, businesses blame the technology crew, who, in turn, blame the system integrator or the software and they, in turn, will find someone else to blame. In this process, no one really learns from the failure, and they start work on the next project, which will probably go the same way.

Design thinking is a useful methodology that can be adapted for multiple situations. Simply put, design thinking is a non-linear, iterative process that focuses on the user and allows for failure. It's a process that is most useful to tackle problems that are ill-defined or unknown. While design thinking is mainly associated with team projects, it can also be easily applied to individual quests. In other words, design thinking is a mindset and a set of procedures that promote analytical and critical thinking in problem solving. Design thinking is about how you think, not what you know. Since design thinking views the process as a journey, the destination or end solution is less important. The design thinking approach offers a technique to address the underlying causes of many failures, such as bad communication, rigid thinking, teams operating in information silos, leadership and so on.

The following principles of design thinking can help whether you are solving a problem on your own or doing so as part of a larger team:

Keep the user in mind: We often get to solving problems without having the user in mind. If we reframe the problem in a human-centric way, it is then possible to uncover new ways to meet user needs. One of the tenets of design thinking is understanding and addressing the needs of the user, i.e., the person you are designing for and who is going to use your product or solution.

Have a multi-disciplinary approach: A problem often requires going beyond the subject matter at hand. If you bring in knowledge from various disciplines or have people in your team from multiple disciplines, the collective knowledge of the team will be greater than the sum of its parts. The Wright brothers closely studied bird wings as passionately as ornithologists, and then used the ideas for wing designs. This is often called a T-shaped approach—a broad understanding of multiple subjects along with deep expertise in one area. One of the primary goals in solving a problem is called DFV, which is a design that Delights the users, is technologically Feasible and economically Viable. However, don't make the team too big. When putting together teams, follow the two-pizza rule—you should not have more people in the team than two pizzas can feed. Bigger teams end up with wasted resources as some people end up becoming supervisors, telling others what to do and getting in the way.

Pre-mortem versus post-mortem: A pre-mortem workshop is one of the exercises you can do at the planning stage. In a pre-mortem workshop, people visualize all the possible things that could go wrong with a project. They do this by imagining that the project has already failed and are now analysing the reasons for failure. It gives everyone the opportunity to look at various risks and mitigate some of them. You will mostly find the usual list of suspects—unclear objectives, lack of communication, low training and so on. A pre-mortem is better than sitting around doing a post-mortem after a failure has occurred.

Have a clear vision: If your vision involves putting a rocket on the moon, be sure to tell everyone about this. People love listening to stories and seeing the larger picture. If people don't see the larger objectives, they might do their individual tasks well, but the larger objective might fail because they don't see the connection between the tasks they are doing and the outcome that is being visualized. Sometimes failure happens because of very small details that someone would have seen if they had known the larger vision. If people have the outcome in mind, people keep it in mind while performing their tasks.

Fail-learn-fail-cycle: In design thinking, failure is built into the process. If you fail early and often, the result is much stronger. It's far better to consider multiple alternatives and test them out rather than sticking to one.

Prototyping: A key process in the design thinking method is to prototype everything in a way that is cost-effective and quick. This encourages you to focus on what is known as opposed to what is said. Prototypes are simple to make. The Wright brothers made hundreds of prototypes, as did Edison. Some could be just drawings or paper cut-outs. Others could be functioning working models. Advancements in 3-D printing allow you to make quick prototypes out of a drawing, and these are great for analysis and learning.

* * *

The Museum of Failure is a travelling exhibition hosting a collection of failed products and services from around the world. The museum first opened in Sweden and has travelled the world as a touring exhibition, visiting different cities with its growing collection of over 200 artefacts. Many innovation projects fail, and the museum showcases these failures to provide visitors with a fascinating insight into the process of creation. Every item provides unique insight into the risky business of innovation and the need to accept failure. The museum aims to stimulate productive discussion about failure and inspire us to take meaningful risks. The museum is curated by Dr Samuel West, a psychologist who wanted all of us to learn from failure.

Handling failure, whether professional or personal, requires effort. You need to have the strength to accept the outcome, the intelligence to learn and the resilience to actionize learning to try again. Failure teaches us several things.

First, it changes your way of thinking and fosters creativity. The route we traditionally associate with success may not work and you might have to take a novel path or step back to try again. This requires creativity. Starting a new career or a new business after failure will require unconventional and unfamiliar methods.

Secondly, failure teaches you about people. People respond differently to situations of success and failure, especially failure in one's career. You also realize who you should work with and whom to avoid based on how they react to the two situations. Success attracts a different set of people to you. Only when you fail do you get to realize who your true friends and advisors are.

Thirdly, failure improves you as a person. You learn to tune out the nonconstructive, negative feedback that comes from failing. You learn to trust yourself and build on your confidence. Failure is painful, but it builds resilience, which gives you the confidence to get up and try again. Often, how you handle failure is more important than the failure itself. The approach you take, your demeanour, your composure, etc. in times of failure matter. Taking responsibility and bringing the right emotional intelligence and maturity are necessary steps in determining success in the next attempt.

Finally, failure tells you what to do differently.[5] If you can identify the steps that led to your failure and why they had the results they did, you can form a strategy for future success.

Chapter 8

Playing the Long Game

I've learned that the long game is the shortcut.

—Richie Norton

Early in my career, I was a part of a sales team tasked with selling racking systems to large industrial plants. From these colleagues, I learnt about the art of selling and building client relationships. Since I was new to the team, I benefited from observing them in action without prior knowledge of their sales technique. I noticed two distinct styles in terms of how they managed a client relationship. The first group believed in putting in time and effort to build long-term relationships with clients, and they had endless patience to go through multiple visits and meetings at client offices, most of which did not seem to yield any results. In some cases, the client did not even have an immediate requirement for the product we were selling. The second category of team members would be focused on closing sales that were immediate. They could sense when a client was ready to place an order, would pounce on the opportunity like a hawk and practically camp at the client office if needed, until they brought the deal to closure.

In terms of results, both groups seemed to have had equal success at the end of the year. But if you looked deeper, the ones who focused on long-term relationships had a much smoother ride in their sale closures. Moreover, their clients rarely considered going to a competitor; in some cases, the clients would even reveal the exact specifications and prices quoted by the competition. These salespeople would also be successful in getting repeat business for the company over time. While the people who focused on the short term did succeed sometimes, the ones who focused on the long term had consistent success.

Success in our careers has a similar trajectory. Some of us approach careers with a short-term plan and achieve early successes, but people who work with a long-term plan usually end up having a more satisfactory career.

Understanding your long-term career goals and how each milestone or touchpoint along the way will help you get closer to achieving them will be critical in shaping your career. If you think short-term, you are going to push to achieve immediate goals and these results may not suit you the best. Besides, in this process, you might miss out on some steps that could be essential building blocks for future opportunities. What is important to acknowledge is that while you may get a particular role, you may not be ready for it and/or it may not be the right option. Further, you might have missed a crucial step that would have enhanced your prospects for something better in the future.

Careers, among many things in the world around us, have become those of quick fulfilment. We can obtain or satisfy a large portion of our consumers' needs instantly. We have delivery services that fulfil our orders within half an hour. We have access to instant entertainment options. We can buy a car or a house much faster than our parents could. Similarly, when it comes to a career, there are options that can serve our needs quickly, especially at the early stage of our careers. You might have friends who look for alternate jobs if their current company doesn't seem to enable their aspirations. Some would have changed six jobs in five years and then hit a plateau in terms of future prospects. At middle levels, hiring becomes more nuanced and consistent performance becomes more important. This is when the luck with short-term career success often runs out.

Here's a scenario that I'd like to share with you. I knew two students who graduated from business school the same year. Both were strong candidates and would have got easily placed in reputed companies. By coincidence, both students were placed during campus placements in the same company and started their working lives a few months later as part of the management training batch. This particular company had a training programme that gave the batch exposure to different businesses so that they could then make an informed choice as to which division they would like to join once their training was complete.

The first student negotiated his future role in the company during the campus placement interview itself, extracting a promise that he would be placed in a division and a location of his choosing. The company, too, seemed willing to agree to this request. After the initial training period, he is appointed to his preferred division that sells consumer electronics and is placed in Hyderabad. He is the only person from the batch who gets into this division, and it seems to the others in the batch that his approach is the right way. On the face of it, it does appear that he seemed to have negotiated and got a good deal, which was deemed a success by the rest of the batch.

The second student goes through the training period designed by the company, spends time learning about the various divisions of the company and interacts with various managers who present different aspects of their business models. He takes his time to understand the various career options available to him. Finally, after some thought, he ends up signing up for a lesser-known division of the company. This choice is not as glamorous, and he is perceived as coming up second best in the career lottery.

Now, this division has just been allotted a new dynamic general manager with a brief to grow the business. Since the division is growing fast and is short of experienced managers, the trainee gets to work on assignments that someone of his experience level would not easily get in other divisions. In a short time, he gets to work on major accounts as a client partner, and based on his performance, he is considered someone who can be promoted to a higher role. He ends up being the first in his training batch to become a sales manager.

While we can attribute some part of the second student's success to luck, this was clearly a long-term approach. He carefully considered options, deliberately choosing the path that would fit his long-term objectives of learning fast and getting the opportunity to front-end with customers. He chose a lesser-known division because he felt that he would get these opportunities earlier. Success usually comes to those who are too busy to look for it. As for the first student who went to Hyderabad, he soon left for another company after a year. Thereafter, he changed a few more jobs in quick succession before finally reaching a career plateau. He came to me for advice at that point, as companies had stopped finding him an attractive hire due to the multiple roles he had done for short periods of time.

The two students in the above story are real people, except that I have slightly changed the details to protect their privacy. But you will find similar situations across companies. Among various tasks, one of my responsibilities was to induct fresh engineering graduates into the company. Since many of them became close acquaintances over the years, I have had a ringside view of their early choices and how their careers progressed. An entry-level engineer usually has to decide three things: the technology to work on, the location of posting and the business unit. Only a few of them thought about the long term and focused on technology, putting the other choices second. Most were focused on getting a location of their choice, and they spent considerable energy in this pursuit. When I look at their career trajectory over a decade, the first group has had better careers.

Getting quick results on our choices gives us a dopamine hit. You would have experienced this during your campus placements or early promotions. But over time, these quick wins will not be as frequent, and you will feel stagnation in your career. We don't tend to view a career as something for the long term and try to artificially accelerate its progress. This does not always work and leaves you with the feeling that something did not quite go the way it was expected to. In case you need to change your company, developing a sound strategy will help you identify the right choice in terms of role. You will then have continuity in terms of the path towards your long-term objective instead of taking a blind leap of faith.

Developing a Career Plan

The 2023 film *The Long Game* tells us the story of a group of Mexican–American high school students in Texas—Joe Treviño, Gene Vasquez, Felipe Romero, Mario Lomas and Lupe Felan—and their love of golf. Denied the privilege of playing on the town's golf course, they forged their own makeshift course in a nearby field and began to play together. Regardless of the initial ridicule they faced, they soon began winning tournaments. They were labelled 'The Mustangs'. They first won local trophies and soon defied all odds to win at the state and national levels.

Their love for the game is what drove them, but their courage to stand up for what they believed in mattered even more. They had a long-term view of how to make golf more accessible for those who didn't come from a privileged background. In 2012, the Mustangs were inducted into the Latino International Sports Hall of Fame for their historic victory. They inspired others to play the game in the 1950s, and their legacy continues today, thanks to *The Long Game*.

Let's look at how to develop a career plan with the long term in mind. A career plan, at its most basic level, is a list of your short-term and long-term goals and the actions you can take to achieve them. This helps you make decisions about the jobs you need to take up, the skills you need to acquire, the cross-functional initiatives you need to sign up for, the networks you need to build and the time you need to invest in areas outside your work. It's good to have this plan written down so that you can visit it periodically and make course corrections as needed.

Some steps to develop a career plan:

1. **Identify what you want to do:** Develop a list of options that fit your profile by examining your interests, skills and values that matter to you. Some of your choices will be based on your qualifications and the available opportunities, but there are always achievable alternatives, even if they appear to be

off the regular path. For example, I know quite a few good software engineers who came into the profession without any prior training. It's important that you understand what motivates you and what will make you happy if you choose a particular career path. Write down the following four things that are the building blocks of identifying what you want: your motivation (what makes you happy); your interests (what do you love to do); your values (what is important to you) and your skills (what are you good at). There will be a set of jobs that fall at the intersection of these four that you should look at as your set of choices.

2. **Prioritize among your choices:** You will now have a list of options in terms of what you want to do. It's now time to prioritize these choices based on your personal situation. For example, if you have chosen a career option that requires certain skills and you are not close, then you need to choose an option that will help you build those skills while enabling you to earn a living. At the early stage of your career, you might want to prioritize financial security or paying back a student loan. Or you may want to work under a specific mentor who teaches at a university that's not your first choice. Prioritizing helps you choose based on relevant criteria.
3. **Create alternatives and compare them:** You should compare your most promising options against alternatives to make the best decision. In 2005, Steve Jobs gave the commencement speech at Stanford. What struck me from his speech was how he made alternate choices during his student life and how these choices helped him achieve what he

did. He explains how sometimes the dots connect only while looking backwards and how you must trust your judgement that these dots will connect. Each option we choose has its own unique benefits and unless you list them down and evaluate them dispassionately, you could end up making choices that don't connect.

4. **Consider larger factors:** You should consider factors beyond your own preferences. We are living in a complex world and even with the best forecasts, things could go awry. For example, consider future prospects and new disruptors in your chosen field. Don't hesitate to speak to people who are already in the field, as they can give you valuable information to help you make better choices.

Once you are done completing the four steps outlined above, make a decision. You could choose more than one option if you are at an early stage of your career. By going through the above process, you will not end up choosing a career path based on your qualifications or what others tell you to do. Career paths are not linear, and a career plan is like a map that offers you alternate routes to reach your long-term goals. Some routes may not be straightforward or could take longer, but as long as you have planned well, they will get you to your goal.

Once you have identified your career option and the path to achieving it, you need to do the following:

- Set specific milestones and timelines to track your progress. This timeline is an indicator and not an absolute. For example, if you want to be a manager in five years, doing it in six or seven years is also perfectly acceptable.

- You should define the parameters for your own success. Avoid focusing on the opinions of others or setting goals based on their performance. It's quite possible that someone might have a better designation or salary, as this is usually relative to the kind of industry and the size of the company. Keep your ego at the door and continue working hard.
- Playing the long game means committing to a plan and the work involved. You may need to take on difficult tasks or attend training programmes that require commitment. Like the ace Mexican golfers, you cannot play the long game unless you get up every morning and practise your swing.

It's important to be realistic about your expectations. While you should largely stick to your plan, feel free to amend it as needed based on new information. For example, an industry could be disrupted by a new technology or there might be geographic shifts creating a new demand. If you are playing for the long game, it's necessary to have course corrections at specific steps. Be sure to incorporate them into your written plan so that it is available for you to review.

Purpose for the Long-Term

The British explorer Ernest Shackleton was fascinated by the South Pole region and spent his lifetime exploring its frozen wasteland. He participated in three expeditions to the Antarctic and is regarded as one of the key figures of the heroic age of Antarctic exploration. In December 1911, he joined Capt. Robert Scott's expedition in the race to the South Pole. Roald Amundsen won that polar race, and quite a few members of Scott's party, including Scott himself, perished during the return journey. A few years later, Shackleton led a new team with the plan of crossing the frozen continent from sea to sea via the South Pole.

Disaster struck the expedition when Shackleton's ship, the *Endurance*, became trapped in pack ice. The crew then had to abandon the ship and camp on the ice around it. They hoped that the ice would melt enough for them to resume their journey. However, the ship, along with much of their stores, sank in the Weddell Sea off Antarctica on 21 November 1915. The team continued camping on ice, but this was not a long-term solution because the ice was disintegrating. They had to take small boats to a nearby shelter on Elephant Island, where they subsisted on the flesh of seals, penguins and fish.

Shackleton embarked on a perilous sixteen-day journey in a small boat with a team of five men, sailing 800 miles to the closest whaling station, South Georgia, across a dangerous stretch of ocean. Four months later, Shackleton returned to Elephant Island and succeeded in rescuing his remaining crew. The most amazing part of this story is that he did not lose a single member of the expedition. In 1921, Shackleton returned to the Antarctic for another expedition but died of a heart attack while his ship was moored near South Georgia. At his wife's request, he was buried there.

Shackleton's story is about tenacity and persistence over a long period of time in his pursuit of exploring the frozen continent. Not all career paths involve treacherous journeys over sea and ice but nevertheless encounter significant obstacles. Your talent and situation may not always suit your chosen career path or larger developments beyond your control could derail your pursuit. From Shackleton's example, we can identify the key aspects of negotiating a career while encountering obstacles: having a clear sense of your values, having passion for what you choose and doing it with purpose.

Values define your passion and purpose. You can view them as a basket of things that are important to you in life and non-negotiable. For example, one of your values could be not taking credit for the work of others. Another value of yours could be pride in your work and not turning out something substandard. Shackleton desired to explore the unknown but stuck to his values of respecting nature and his team while pursuing his goal.

Write down your values while planning your career. Once you know what your values are, it's easier to make key decisions about your career. As an exercise, start by writing down things in life that are very important to you. The list could include family, environment, service and financial stability. If the value is important to you, put it on the list. Since this list is for you only, be totally honest and if needed, define each value you put in using your own words. You can use the dictionary if you wish, but the definition should be your own. For example, if one of your values is to care for the environment, your specific definition could be to live sustainably and not take more than what you need from planet Earth.

Once you've defined your values, you should use them to guide your career choices. Let's look at an example. If one of your values is the environment, and you are interviewing with an investment bank that, among other things, trades in oil futures, you will then need to decide between a great job and your defined values. You could choose to join the bank and work towards making a change or you could choose an alternate option.

Next comes passion. Passion is what drives you to take on challenging activities that align with your values. Passion is a drive that comes deeply from within, and it's this emotion that drives your commitment to a career. For example, company founders are willing to sacrifice their cushy careers, their savings and their time in pursuit of the single arching passion of creating a company of value. Another way of defining passion is that it is something you will do even without any promise of reward.

Limit your career to one single passion that means the most to you. You could have some other passion outside of your work, like music or cooking, but be clear about the single passion that drives your career choices. A colleague I know had a very promising career in the corporate world, yet his passion was sports. He was deeply passionate about identifying sporting talent in small towns and villages and building it up through professional coaching and facilities. He could find a perfect fit with an upcoming non-profit that was investing in developing sporting talent and he joined it as its CEO.

Finally, there is purpose. At a basic level, purpose is the reason for your existence—a sense of meaning and direction in your life and career. In fact, a good way to find your purpose at work is to ask yourself, 'What do I want to be remembered for after I've left this company?'

You could choose career paths that fit your purpose or use the larger idea as a reference point while making career decisions. A colleague had the purpose of improving people's food choices, especially when it came to milk.

For various reasons, the current method of procuring regular milk leaves some consumers in discomfort. Done in industrial-scale housing with thousands of cattle in less-than-ideal environments, the dairy farms produce significant emissions of greenhouse gases that contribute to climate change. In addition to damaging the environment, it causes animal suffering. Other people have lactose intolerance and would welcome substitutes. His idea was to develop a plant-based milk product that people could use instead of regular milk. He left a steady job to pursue this idea and is doing well in a career that fits his purpose.

In summary, when it comes to your career choices, your values are your foundation, your passion is what will excite and motivate you and your purpose is the reason for your existence. Put all three in alignment, and you could be navigating the Weddell Sea towards the South Pole without a care.

Jobs and Careers

Over the course of your career, you will do several jobs. For this discussion, we will refer to jobs as work assignments that last about a year or so. Your career plan should ideally determine the jobs you will take up throughout your working life. If you have planned your career well, the jobs you take on will be building blocks for your career. Imagine wanting to build a house with a collection of Lego bricks. The bricks are the jobs you will take up and the house is your career. Just as multiple Lego bricks are needed to construct the house, similarly, multiple jobs contribute towards a successful career.

When you apply or interview for a job, it should be towards your long-term objective. If the job you are looking at somehow doesn't fit in the collection of blocks needed to construct your career, you will be better off avoiding it. You cannot build a career expecting odd bricks to somehow fit your plan. This way, you will interview better and explain why the particular job suits you the best and the reason the interviewer should hire you.

A career is a long-term endeavour, something you build on and work towards over time. A job is a short-term endeavour, and you could be taking on several jobs, but remember that it has to be done with the purpose of building up your career through the experiences and learnings it gives you. A good example is in soccer matches where the ball is not necessarily passed in the direction of the goal, but passing sideways or backwards is all part of the play towards scoring a goal.

Playing the long game is quite a well-used strategy in sports.[1] In simple terms, playing the long game means paying a small price today to make things simpler in the future. It can work in both professional and personal dimensions. It required foregoing immediate results to create sustainable change that will hold you in good stead over the long term. On the other hand, going for the short game means going for quick results and putting off difficult things for later, even if they may not be sustainable tomorrow. The short game usually offers instant and noticeable results. This can have tactical advantages at times, but anyone who has achieved anything significant has always played the long game.

So, how do you play the long game when it comes to the various jobs you will take up throughout your career? Long-term career goals can take many different forms. You need to have a clear direction and goal in terms of what you want to achieve and when. This could include a certain job title, leading a certain sized team or becoming an expert in a particular field. Having a clear objective can help you decide what actions you might need to take. For example, becoming an expert in the field might mean that you will take up positions that are difficult or don't pay well for now, but the expertise you pick up will go towards meeting your long-term objective.

It's important to build in alternate scenarios for your job choices. Things change, especially in business. The economic situation could change, a competing product could come in or customer preferences might simply change.[2] All this requires you to build in flexibility with respect to your plans and choice of jobs. One way to play the long game is to work in large companies or job environments. Well-established companies with formal structures and systems have multiple options to offer and have development plans that you could make use of. For example, if marketing is your area of interest and your current job cannot suit that, you could use to rotate internally. Your friend might, however, prefer the start-up world, which has a fast-paced environment. In these places, people usually multitask, get exposure to multiple functions and learn quickly.

A long-term player would plan jobs rather than rush the process. For example, someone who is interested in a start-up would look at whether their purpose mirrors their own. They would research the founding team and see if it were a place they would want to work.

For the purpose of improving your game, it's good to study the career paths of people you would categorize as successful in the areas you have chosen. Their journeys can give you insights to use in your own journey.

Stepping Back to Reflect

When playing the long game, you should reflect on where you are and what you can do next. I have found the end of the financial year is the best time to do this, while some others do it at the end of the calendar year. During this time, you think about what you have accomplished so far, list what was planned but left undone, include new information about your company, job or skills, get feedback from assessments and so on.

Treat this reflection as a formal process and not a casual activity. Some companies make this a part of the review process, but you don't need to wait. Record your thoughts and career goals either on paper or on your laptop or cloud drive so that they can be easily recovered next year. You must make your career plan a living document that is easily accessible to you.

And What about Playing with Others in the Long Game?

An important part of playing for the long term is building your network. Careers are built on connections. The network you build through the years helps open possibilities when you least expect them, and could also help you make the right decisions with timely advice. Think of every interaction you have with others as a possibility to strengthen your network. For example, a conversation on a flight might give you useful knowledge and, if lucky, even lead to a long-term mentoring relationship. Though I wouldn't recommend you annoy people who don't wish to engage, you will be surprised by the success you can get by just asking. Networks nurtured over time lead to outcomes like getting into your dream company, getting a chance at doing something different or having interesting interludes in your career journey.

Expanding your skills or knowledge is another way of building your connections. Pushing yourself to build on your skills or knowledge allows you the ability to demonstrate your desire to do new things and highlight your readiness to grow your career. Never miss the opportunity to sign up for trainings, certifications or courses. Another great way to expand both your knowledge and your connections is through industry conferences that happen in areas of interest. Most are happy to allow you to attend with prior registration, and these are great ways to build knowledge as well as meet people.

Good career advice is so hard to come by, and more importantly, it needs to fit into one's long-term plan. You can make a great deal of difference by giving the right advice to others, especially if you believe in playing the long game. If you are one of those individuals who is living their true potential in the world of work, at some point, it's time to share this with others as a manager, mentor or expert. However, there is an art and science to helping others with useful advice.

The first rule is to avoid giving people unsolicited advice. You will not know their long-term plan, and you could be giving advice that boosts your own confidence in what you are doing. Also, your knowledge might be outdated, and the context and circumstances might be different.

Secondly, focus on the situation at hand. Advice is useful if it is adapted to the user's situation. For example, if you are advising a colleague about applying to an internal job posting, do consider their strengths and weaknesses and their fit for the role. If the role is demanding and the individual's personal situation cannot accommodate the demands, they might be overlooking something that you can clearly see. Don't be afraid to call that out. If someone is setting out on a job search after a layoff, place yourself in their situation and empathize with what they are going through. Your advice will then be far more relevant.

The biggest service you can provide someone in their career journey is helping them figure out what they need for themselves. Your role should be that of a partner or sounding board that helps them think through their situation. I recently partnered with a former colleague who had just lost his job. He couldn't figure out why he found himself in the situation he was in. While he had initially approached me with the goal of making some contacts with search firms, it was a short-term approach. We spent time together working out the reasons for the job loss and his strengths that he should play to. By doing this analysis, he could figure out for himself which jobs he should apply to and which to avoid. He is now employed in a new organization that better aligns with his strengths.

It's also important not to give any advice that may cause more bad than good. There are a lot of people who have ended up in wrong careers because they got bad advice when they sought it. If you don't have something useful to offer, stay silent. You could point them to others who might be more helpful in the situation.

When the Game Doesn't Go Your Way

Let's face it—not all goals will be achieved the first time and unforeseen obstacles will arise. Rejection is a natural part of building our careers. Even during the down times, you can play the long game with your attitude and how you handle adversity. Even if you run into some challenges in achieving your career goal, remember that you can use the process and experience as key learning. You can understand what didn't go well, how you can improve, what ways you can continue nurturing your relationships and pivot if you need to. With careful planning, intention, patience and a positive attitude, you can achieve your career goals.

For a long time, careers followed a predictable path—you joined a reputed company, worked hard and over time moved up the ladder. Companies no longer maintain this path, rendering it unreliable. Companies must adapt their business model to the demands of the marketplace, leading to the expectation that individuals largely control careers. Career ladders are being replaced by what is termed career lattices, where your progress may be diagonal, horizontal or even reverse. Guidance from companies on how to move forward in this environment is often minimal because they just aren't sure. Increasingly, they're relying on individual professionals to take more active control of their careers. Playing the long game can help you succeed in the world. It doesn't matter in what direction the ball moves as long as the strategy ends up with you netting more goals.

Now, let's take a moment to chart a long-term career plan:

My Career Development Plan

Personal Vision Statement What you hope to achieve in your career over the next five years.

Values, Passion and Purpose

List out your guiding principles and what you're looking for in your career.

My values are:

What I am passionate about:

What would I like to be remembered for:

Career Goals or Measurable Career Milestones	
Short-Term	**Long-Term**

Personal Reflections

Strengths / Weaknesses	Growth / Learning Opportunities
What I am good at and will help me towards my career goals / What could delay me?	What should I learn and build skills on What are the new jobs I could volunteer for
•	•
•	•
•	•

Action Plan for Year 1		
Career Goal	Action Items	Completion Date
1.	•	
2.	•	
3.	•	

Action Plan for Years 2–5		
Career Goal	Action Items	Completion Date
1.	•	
2.	•	
3.	•	

Chapter 9

Doing the Right Things Right

The softest pillow is a clear conscience.

—N.R. Narayana Murthy

On the morning of 29 October 2018, Lion Air flight 610 took off from Jakarta's main airport on a routine domestic flight with 189 people on board. Just thirteen minutes into the flight, the plane crashed into the Java Sea, killing everyone on board. The flight was operated on a Boeing 737 MAX aircraft, a model that had been introduced into commercial flying just about a year before. There seemed to be no warnings from the pilot or the engineering crew before the crash. Preliminary investigations using data from the aircraft's flight recorders revealed very odd aircraft behaviour that indicated control problems that could be associated with the flight's computer systems. It seemed as if the computer was behaving contrary to what the pilots were trying to do. After the crash, corrective guidelines and warnings were issued to all operators of this series of aircraft by the manufacturer. However, no fundamental changes were made to the programming or operation of the computers that controlled the aircraft's avionics.

A few months later, in March 2019, Ethiopian Airlines flight 302 crashed under eerily similar circumstances—a short while into flight with no warning given of any trouble. The behaviour of this aircraft, again a 737 MAX, seemed very similar to that of the Lion Air flight. A second crash of the same type of aircraft within a space of a few months was too much of a coincidence, and regulators across the world reacted quickly. Countries across the world ordered the grounding of all 737 MAX aircraft in operation. This caused billions of dollars in losses to the industry, most of which were borne by the manufacturer, Boeing. The estimated loss is about $60 billion. There were close to 1200 cancelled orders for the 737 MAX model.

However, this action was too late for the 300 people who boarded these two flights, just like millions do around the world every day, trusting their lives to the machines and the hands of the men and women who fly them. Why was the trust misguided this time?

A detailed investigation identified that the key reason for the two crashes was the aircraft's Manoeuvring Characteristics Augmentation System (MCAS). This is a flight stabilizing feature that was developed especially by Boeing for this model. While the 737 series of aircraft had been in operation for more than fifty years, the 737 MAX was larger than the earlier versions. Due to its longer length and engine position, the nose of the aircraft tended to move up during certain flight manoeuvres. In simple terms, the plane's airframe had crossed the limits and needed to be corrected. There were two possible approaches to address this particular problem. The conventional way would have been to redesign the airframe; the second would have been by introducing a software-controlled correction system to the flight controls.

Changing the airframe design would have taken too long and cost money. This would also entail testing and certifying the aircraft. Boeing was in a hurry to launch an aircraft to compete with its rival Airbus, which had just introduced the A321neo model that had already attracted attention from airlines worldwide. Many airline chiefs had indicated to Boeing in private that they would order new planes from Airbus unless there was a competing model from the Boeing stable.

As a result, Boeing chose a software solution to correct the problem. This solution did prove effective in test situations and seemed to be a viable option. This allowed Boeing to launch the plane as a variant of the 737 family. This saved time in terms of redesign, testing, certification and pilot training. It seemed like a great idea, except that no one foresaw all possible scenarios that could happen, including what happened in the two tragic flights to terrain.

The MCAS was a computer-based compensatory control system that countered the tendency of the nose to go up by correcting it downward. However, the MCAS was not tested rigorously as needed and several scenarios were missed in the test phase. Most importantly, the early flight manuals used by pilots did not have a full description of the MCAS system or clear instructions on how to disable this system if needed. Even more worrying was that after the Lion Air accident, pilots and airlines, including Ethiopian Airlines, were not effectively trained about the MCAS and its operation.

It was later evident that MCAS played a key role in both accidents. The FAA then ordered design changes for each MAX aircraft, which included additional controls and triggers for MCAS activation and allowed pilots to override the system based on their situational judgment.

It also required all pilots to undergo MCAS simulator training, especially for adverse occurrences.

Post-accident investigations also revealed organizational issues at Boeing that seemed to have contributed. These issues are common in many companies, primarily a clash between the commercial divisions and the engineering divisions. Intra-company mail exchanges showed that some Boeing designers had expressed concern about this particular model of the aircraft. Engineers at the plant had raised safety concerns about the larger airframe and engine imbalances. In fact, one of them had written a prophetic memo that said, 'And for the first time in my life, I'm sorry to say that I'm hesitant about putting my family on a Boeing airplane.'

Over the years, Boeing has always enjoyed a stellar reputation as an engineering icon. Engineers with a passion for technical work in specialized fields competed to work for Boeing. The company's engineering culture goes back to its founder, William Boeing. A perfectionist in engineering and safety, he pioneered the era of cost-effective yet safe civil aviation. A culture of safety and customer comfort had resulted in Boeing launching several successful models of aircraft—the 737 and the 747 in the 1960s, and more recently, the 777 and 787 series. All these models have outstanding safety records, and millions of passengers trust their lives every day on Boeing planes around the world.

However, over the years, there seemed to be a change in culture at Boeing. It seemed like a gradual shift away from safety, engineering and design to quick profits and commercial gains. What was forgotten is that in a high-profile industry like commercial aviation, a single accident can destroy value and reputation built over years.

According to an investigation report, priorities went wrong at Boeing. The urgency to compete with Airbus and launch an aircraft model that was not fully ready resulted in the company focusing on the wrong things. Doing things right would have meant allowing designers to design and test the plane, for engineers to give their inputs and for pilots to extensively test and train on the new model. It would have meant a few more months of launch delays and some loss in sales, but no loss in terms of lives or reputation. As for Boeing, the learning is ongoing. The 737MAX is again certified to fly after various fixes, but some new problems have emerged.[1] If you don't do things the right way, the fix takes longer.

There are other such examples where individuals and companies choose quick gains over doing the right things. We need to recognize the path we take on our individual journeys. In an organization, individuals subsume their identity to the larger corporate direction or decision. We have all been exposed to what is termed situational influence, where, because of the situation, we either do wrong or mostly look the other way when we see wrong. And the moment to do right quickly passes by.

Dilemmas Faced by Humans at Work

Ethics are moral principles that govern our behaviour. While ethics are not limited to the workplace, we will look at some situations that are common to the workplace and see how you can navigate them in this chapter. You can apply the same learnings outside the office.

Situations where we are conflicted between what we would like to do as individuals and what we seem to be asked to do as part of an organizations are frequent. They can be termed workplace dilemmas. They are called dilemmas because there is usually no right solution, but we have choices to make. Many times, the situation doesn't offer a great outcome, whichever way you choose. For example, you might find a friend at work frequently gaming the attendance system to show that he is in the office while being somewhere else. If you reported this issue, the office, of course, would quickly correct the situation, but then that could mean the end of your friendship.

Other examples include making use of internal information to trade in the company's stock, getting a relative out of turn employment in the company, using the company's resources for personal use and so on. The question is the same—doing the right thing right. You could find yourself in two positions. You could either be the person making the decisions or a witness to someone else doing wrong. The first step is understanding the dilemma and then applying ethical principles consistently. To get a better understanding of how ethical dilemmas present themselves, let's look at the famous trolley problem that has been used for teaching ethics over the years.

The trolley problem is formulated to spur a debate by presenting us with several dilemmas built around the scenario of a runaway trolley train hurtling down a track where several people are working. There are many creative variations of this problem centred on the decision you are faced with.

Let's take the most basic version of the dilemma: a trolley barrelling down the tracks. Ahead, on the tracks, there are five people who cannot move, and the trolley is headed straight for them. You are standing at a distance in the train yard, next to a lever. If you pull this lever, the trolley will switch to a different set of tracks. However, you notice that there is one person on the side track. You have ONLY two options:

1. Do nothing; in which, case the trolley will kill all five people on the main track.
2. Pull the lever, diverting the trolley onto the side track, where it will kill one person.

The problem can be made infinitely more complex by stating that the one person on the side track is your son or that the five people working on the main track are your friends and so on.

Which is the more ethical option? Or, more simply, what is the right thing to do? Before you go forward, take a moment to think about what you would do. It's important that you choose your answer before reading the next paragraph.

Your decision: ______________________________

Some of us would choose the option to save as many lives as possible. To give you a workplace analogy, you find similar solutions coming up in offices when the decision to reduce the workforce comes up for discussion. By asking a few people to leave the company, you will end up saving many jobs. People view this action as being for the greater good.

Another set of people will say that it's not justified to throw the switch to kill one worker and save many lives. Assume that the larger set of workers were not permitted by rules to be on the main track. They disregarded the rules and went there anyway, putting themselves in danger.

A smaller third group will say that they are observers and are not obliged to make a decision. There are some folks in the office too who don't get involved, even if they observe things and could intervene to make change.

The trolley problem, like most philosophical questions, has no definitive solution. I used it in this chapter to provoke thought and appreciation of the limitations of resolving ethical dilemmas. But it does not mean that decision-making is not possible in this situation. We can reasonably resolve the questions we face at work through reasoning and rational problem-solving using available data. Not everyone might agree with the solution, but by removing individual preferences and emotions out of the solution, you can still arrive at a decision, which is what you need to do in a work setting.

While we may not face decisions about someone dying as a result of our actions or inaction, we do face issues that require us to make the right decisions. Sometimes the decision might appear to be minor and inconsequential. However, when it comes to doing the right thing, there is no minor decision, as how you decide on minor issues has consequences in the long run. A series of wrong decisions will add up and lead to a serious situation later. For example, ignoring minor frauds in expense accounts could eventually lead to an inaccurate projection of the entire sales revenue forecast. Some members of the team would have extended their practice of making minor adjustments to their expense claims to adjust the sales numbers they were reporting. In a factory, overlooking minor safety violations will one day lead to a major accident as the culture of safety gets eroded by the neglect of minor issues.

One variation to the trolley problem is introducing a personal element, stating that either the lone worker or the group is related to you. In office settings, some of us may make different decisions based on our relationships with the affected party. In one of the companies I was associated with, a senior member of the leadership team had a physical relationship with a co-worker. A well-wisher conveyed this to the CEO, who chose to ignore this information because the individual in question was a star performer and a friend. A year later, the company faced a sexual harassment lawsuit and ended up paying out a huge settlement.

The key is to not let distractions such as office relationships, personal views, situational constructs, etc., come in the way of making the right decisions. It's important to recognize an ethical issue when it presents itself and be conscious that you are making a decision on something that has relevance beyond the immediate situation.

Here are some tips on how to go about making decisions to do the right things the right way:

1. **Consider the principles at risk:** You need to first ask yourself what value or principle is being violated. In the airplane example, the principle at risk was the operation of a plane carrying passengers without the necessary checks being carried out. Also look at whether it's something important to you personally or impacting the company as well. For example, if your colleague clocks out early every day, one might consider that a short-changing of company time. If your co-worker routinely meets goals and completes their work, someone else might not see the situation as an ethical concern. You personally might not like someone leaving before time, but it doesn't seem to impact the company. However, it might not always be so simple. By leaving early,

there could be something left undone that could cause a problem later. Before bringing the matter to someone's attention, assess the risk to find clarity on the issue. If you ultimately find it too risky, consider taking action.

2. **Have a conversation with your fellow workers:** It's a good idea to talk to fellow employees whenever possible. In the airplane example, a group of design engineers could have discussed their concerns openly and even invited their supervisors to the discussion. Start the discussion by asking questions and allowing them to respond. This is a reasonably safe way to start a discussion without accusing someone. It's possible that there might be an explanation that you missed or that the point of concern has already been addressed. If not, the discussion will spur thinking and bring the concern into the open, where it can be better dealt with.
3. **Refer to the company handbook or training material:** Most organizations have an employee handbook outlining professional conduct and behaviour expected at work. Check the chapter on ethics to figure out what action you could take and how to go about it. If you have access to a compliance and ethics hotline, use it to discuss or highlight your concern. If allowed, you can anonymously report misconduct or corporate ethics violations. Whistle-blowing is now a protected activity in many countries.[2] Some people prefer this option rather than reporting directly to leadership to reduce any concerns about retaliation. Referring to codes of conduct and ethics can help you determine what steps to take when solving challenging moral

dilemmas. Similar to a company's own ethics hotline, many industries have one of their own. For example, you can report a lawyer's ethics violation to the state bar association or a company's matter to the registrar of companies or securities board.

4. **Trust your instincts:** Many times, when you sense something isn't right at work, it's often worth exploring rather than ignoring. This can help protect both your company and yourself in the event of any unethical activity taking place. Trusting your instincts might also mean you first confirm or investigate your suspicions before taking other actions. For example, you might become more observant of a colleague if you think that they are moonlighting with a second job because their work pattern has changed and they suddenly seem to have extra cash available to spend.
5. **Protect your interests:** Speaking up does not guarantee complete protection against retaliation, regardless of what companies claim. Hence, it's a good idea to take adequate steps to protect your own interests. Some of the things you can do are have some allies, especially at senior levels, and also document the evidence as well as your complaints so that a record is available. The protections provided by law are getting stronger, but they are still inadequate. In some recent cases, individuals who reported violations faced initial consequences before receiving protection against retaliation.

No Right Way to Do the Wrong Thing

Here are two interesting examples of wrongdoing in very large organizations. In 2016, Volkswagen was found using a creative solution to ensure that the cars they sold in the US met the required emission standards. These cars were fitted with a defeat device. This device was actually embedded software that could detect whether the car was being driven on an actual road or on a test bed used to test for emissions. Based on the situation, the software altered the engine performance to improve the emission results. In April 2017, a US federal judge ordered Volkswagen to pay a $2.8 billion fine and its CEO was charged with fraud.[3]

The second case concerns Wells Fargo, a company that's been in business since 1852. In September 2016, Wells Fargo was found opening close to 1.5 million new accounts that were not authorized by customers. This happened over a five-year period. The regulators charged Wells Fargo under various laws and the bank ended up paying a fine of $185 million. Many employees later said that they had contacted the company's ethics hotline to complain, but nothing was done.

These two massive breaches in companies with stellar reputations give a lot of food for thought. Employees and leaders in both companies thought it was all right to bypass internal controls, ignore their stated missions of customer first and concerns of employees, and take actions for short-term gains. It's a slippery slope once your employees start chasing profits and quarterly results.

And it's not always a group that does wrongdoing. In November 2023, Sam Bankman–Fried, the founder of the crypto currency exchange FTX, was convicted of fraud and money laundering by a New York jury in a landmark criminal verdict that condemned the former crypto tycoon to a 25-year prison term. Once regarded as a celebrity, he enjoyed a cult following and was welcomed at the White House and on Capitol Hill. For many, he was the public face of the cryptocurrency industry and his company attracted billions of dollars in investment. The New York prosecutors accused him of orchestrating one of the biggest financial frauds in American history.

Being honest with oneself is the first step for individuals and companies to do the right thing. You can look at following these simple rules for both yourself and your company:

Start with yourself: Have a personal reflection about your own values and purpose in life. If you wish, you can discuss this with someone who knows you well, like your spouse or mentor. Don't be afraid to question your assumptions about what matters to you. Some of your life choices, such as career, spouse, friends, etc., will help you understand what most matters to you. Once you have done that, you could choose to have a conversation with your team about what matters to them the most so that there is congruence. It's a good idea to document your purpose and values as a note to yourself that you can revisit when faced with decision-making involving ethical issues.

Be prepared to run into obstacles: Throughout your career, you will face pressures that will question your choices and assumptions. It could be manager expectations, your own aspirations, or even shareholder expectations. There is always a gap between what we want to do and what we end up doing. Being true to your values will sometimes mean that you will run into headwinds in terms of your career or financial progression in the short term. Don't lose your patience when this happens, as no one has established a personal value system without running into obstacles. The same goes for companies. During my time at Infosys, the founders of the company would narrate stories that tested each of the values the company espoused, showing how these were not just statements, but forged under a test of heat and pressure. I vividly remember one example. The story goes as follows: the company's largest client wanted a discount that would have hurt the fledgling company. Rather than agree, the founders choose to say no to the ask. However, they took all the necessary steps to ensure a smooth handover and prevented any business disruption for the client. The lesson to learn was that professionalism and client satisfaction come first. This decision set the tone for many future client negotiations and profitable growth.

Keep the lines of communication open across levels: In most companies, employees at the lower level fear speaking the truth to leaders about things that they observe and don't find ethical. These people can often give you advance information about the misalignment between purpose and values. There are many ways to do this depending on your comfort. The easiest one is to be approachable at every level and give people confidence that their reporting is confidential. Consider what the leaders at Wells Fargo or Boeing would have learned if they had kept communication lines open with the lower levels of the organization.

If you aspire to lead ethically and with high purpose, you must consistently have these honest conversations with yourself and your team. Be prepared to run into obstacles as well be approachable to everyone. If you are a team member aspiring to lead one day, you can follow these very same principles.

Do Machines Need to Have Ethics?

In 1942, science fiction author Isaac Asimov introduced a set of rules so that robots and humans could work together. There were no robots then, but the rules are simple and universal. They are as follows:

- **The First Law:** A robot may not injure or, through inaction, allow a human being to come to harm.
- **The Second Law:** A robot must obey the orders given to it by human beings, except where such orders would conflict with the First Law.
- **The Third Law:** A robot must protect its own existence as long as such protection does not conflict with the First or Second Law.

The next generations of generative AI, quantum computing, and other emerging technologies don't just pose a challenge for organizational operations and strategy; they also raise thorny ethical questions that can impact the way we work and society at large. Today, neither businesses nor individuals are equipped to handle these challenges. For example, can we predict what solution an AI-based system would come up with when faced with the trolley problem? Whether we like it or not, such systems will soon have decision-making capabilities that could put the human at work in danger.

Today, generative AI tools are poised to change the way every business and individual operate. We need to do something new and different to avoid the biggest risks from systems that learn on their own. We need to talk about machine ethics in clear, direct terms, including difficult situations that go against Asimov's laws. We need to outline how an organization could introduce systems responsibly, how to prevent harmful bias from proliferating in recruiting systems, how to avoid key privacy risks and much more. AI tools are creating a whole new world of opportunity and risk, and we need to understand this better.

In October 2021, Frances Haugen, a former Facebook[4] employee, in her testimony before the US Congress, claimed that Facebook's products harmed children, stoked divisions in society and weakened democracy. What was more worrying was her claim that the company knew about these risks and chose to largely ignore them to protect profits. Facebook's own internal research, she claimed, demonstrated just how dangerous the company's products are, and yet the company did little to change or put in place safeguards, fearful of compromising its business model.

She also told Congress that Facebook had the ability to better regulate its products and effectively prevent the platform from being used for illegal activities. She claimed that it has the capacity to identify underage users, present content with filters and prevent the spread of dangerous misinformation. Facebook's algorithm, Haugen said, organized content based on engagement, which could lead to the most inflammatory and shocking posts getting preferential treatment and moving their way to the top of any given person's feed. Essentially, the company (or its programme) made decisions about what it wanted you to see, and it kept the reason for those decisions secret from the public. What is concerning is that many of the decisions seemed to happen automatically based on algorithms, without a human in charge.

Many companies are investing in AI-driven systems. There is a need to have a view of ethical AI both at individual and company level. The risks range from faulty and discriminatory facial recognition to privacy violations and to random profiling interview candidates. AI-based systems bring about many new areas that we need to be concerned about, and companies need to address these risks through greater awareness and mitigation strategies.

Dealing with AI ethical risks is not very different from dealing with other technology-induced risks. You need to extend your ethics programme to include AI risks and raise awareness across levels so that individuals can actively look for such risks in their day-to-day activities. It's crucial to ensure that every employee knows the risks and participates in the decisions that need to be made on the right usage of new technologies. Employees need to know how those risks impact their own jobs and how they fit into the company's values. For example, one area that is highly susceptible to AI-based risk is the recruitment process. Most recruitment software now has an inbuilt AI engine that selects and filters candidates. However, these systems are prone to selection bias, and a company would end up missing some critical hires by relying on them. A recruiter who is aware of such risks could place guardrails for bias and take corrective action. Similar to aircraft MCAS, sometimes it's necessary to disable the auto system and use manual controls.

Another example is how companies gather data about you when you interact with their sites as a customer. Most companies say that they respect privacy yet allow your data to go out either deliberately or through weak systems. You need to tie intent to guardrails. For example, you can have rules like the data owner will always anonymize data when sharing it with third parties. Such rules will first communicate clearly to the team both the risks and the rules for operation. Sometimes, having simple rules around ethics removes the need for people to exercise discretion. When values are articulated and communicated in a way that ties them to actions and there are consequences for not following those rules, then the chances of people doing wrong on their own reduce significantly.[5]

Creating an Ethical Map for Yourself

Now is the time to focus on us. Let's try and prepare a map that will help us navigate a world that's getting increasingly complex when it comes to situations we face. Let's look at three goals for navigation. You can imagine them as the three axes that you used for drawing geometric shapes in school.

- Being happy in one's chosen career (X-axis)
- Being content with your relationships—spouse, family, friends (Y-axis)
- How to not do things that will cause harm?[6] (Z-axis)

Frederick Herzberg was an American psychologist who was especially known for his work on motivation. One of his findings was that the greatest motivator in our lives is not money but the opportunity to learn and grow in our jobs. We all aspire to contribute to a larger goal and be recognized for our achievements. You can verify this by comparing how you feel about yourself when you have a great day at work to how you feel when you have a bad day. On a happy day, you will be able to bring the above ingredients into your job—the ability to constantly learn, regular progression in your career and being recognized, valued and known for your integrity.

The second aspect is ensuring a healthy relationship with your family and friends. I have interacted with people I have known for over two decades or more. Some I have either worked with in the past, others I have known in college. Some are full of energy and happy; others are unhappy and feel alienated from their spouse or children. If we were to go back in time, neither they nor I could have predicted who would end up in which category, but it has clearly something to do with their individual purpose and choices.

Rarely do we choose to invest any extra time we have into our relationships—with spouse, with children, with friends. Most of us have this unconscious habit to underinvest in our families and overinvest in our careers—even though families and friends can be the most powerful and enduring source of happiness that stay with us long after our career is over.

If you study the root causes of some of the business disasters I have covered in this chapter, you will find a common thread of how people, especially leaders, focused on immediate gratification. If you look at personal lives through that lens, you'll see the same pattern when things don't work out in terms of personal success. You will have people allocating fewer and fewer resources to the things that matter most.

On 28 January 1986, the Space Shuttle Challenger exploded seventy-three seconds after lift-off, killing all seven crew members. Subsequent failure analysis revealed that the disaster was caused by the failure of an O-ring, a circular gasket that cost very little. The O-ring sealed the gap in the rocket booster and prevented fuel from leaking. This had failed due to the low temperature (31°F or -0.5°C) on that particular launch day—a risk that several engineers noted but that NASA management dismissed as a marginal risk. The right decision would have been to delay the launch until the weather warmed up. What seemed to be a small problem in the beginning became a big problem later.

To avoid getting into trouble, one must avoid letting small problems grow into bigger ones. You will find that the small ones start off as a shift in snow and add up just like an avalanche on a slippery slope. Often, we ignore small risks that seem marginal. You hear people saying things like, 'I would not allow this exception for most cases, but I will overlook it for this one instance.' Ensure that ignoring something just once doesn't become a regular practice.

What Will You Be Remembered for?

I recently had a conversation with a senior executive I've worked with who is a cancer survivor. Over a long and fulfilling career, he made a tremendous impact on the companies he worked with. What he told me has stayed with me. He said to me that the impact he made on companies seemed very unimportant now. What he was grateful for was the impact he made on individuals whose lives he touched—as a manager, a leader, a father, a colleague, a member of society and so on. Overall, he wanted to be remembered most of all for making a difference to people he met and places he worked, and not doing wrong things, because, in his words, 'there is no right way to do a wrong thing'.

Epilogue

On 24 April 1990, the space shuttle Discovery lifted off from Earth with the Hubble Space Telescope nestled securely in its payload bay. The following day, Hubble was released into space, ready to explore the vast unknown. Since then, Hubble has reinvigorated and reshaped our perception of the cosmos, revealing a universe of unexpected wonders. Hubble has unveiled properties of space and time that scientists and philosophers, for most of human history, could only explore in their imaginations. Today, Hubble continues to provide views of cosmic wonders hitherto not seen and is at the forefront of many new discoveries.

Named after the American astronomer Edwin Hubble, this telescope is the result of international cooperation between the space agencies of several nations. In 1929, Edwin Hubble, through his observations, was the first to describe what is known in physics as the redshift phenomenon. When objects shift away from us at great speeds, the frequency of the light we see shifts towards the red, and when objects move towards us, the light shifts towards the blue. Astronomers use this principle, as well as the terms redshift or blueshift, to define how far galaxies are from us on planet Earth and to give us a sense of the constantly expanding universe.

A similar shift appears to be happening in the workplace. Due to changes in technology, the impact of globalization, new regulations, changes in business models, etc., what was familiar in our world of work seems to be rapidly shifting away from us. We can call this the redshift in the world of work.

At the same time, we see some things coming closer to us. We need to preserve the lessons learnt by humans over years of working together. The focus on the human at the workplace, consciousness towards nature and the environment, communication, managers closely collaborating with people, celebrating milestones, coffee conversations, commuter friends, a shared joy in working together to accomplish objectives, etc. This represents the blueshift.

As humans, we need to balance the redshift and blueshift to get the best out of our work universe. While we cannot fight the expansion of human knowledge, in the evolving landscape of work, adaptability has become a compass for success. As we acknowledge the red shift in the world of work in terms of technology, we need the blue shift in terms of how to build and keep human relationships at work and how we focus on the human in the evolving world of work.

We will do our best work when we give each other the space and the ability to be human at work in a way that is fully human.

During the summer of 2023, as I was planning to leave the familiar landscape of an organization I had been long associated with, I realized that the way of working that I had started out with nearly two decades ago was totally different from what I needed in the future; in essence, I needed to change. Moreover, I felt compelled to distil and share the knowledge I gained from the many years I had spent working with some wonderful colleagues and friends, both in and outside of work. This book is a result of that thought. I hope you find some parts of it useful in your own quest.

The formula for success at work varies for each one of us, but some parts remain: embracing continuous learning, cultivating a growth mindset and leveraging technology as an ally. Over the years, I have seen many successes among the people I have worked with. Their formula comes down to their ability to navigate change with resilience, building and using diverse networks and never underestimating the power of collaboration. More importantly, there are two very personal dimensions: maintaining a healthy work life and never losing sight of their moral compass.

The world around us is going to remain complex, with geopolitical tensions that could snap and challenge us, the impact of climate change on our lives, the damage we have caused by human activity, new technology that is useful and destructive at the same time and a serious shortage of leadership in all places that matter. All this will impact us in a way we cannot imagine.

When new technologies emerge, they benefit different groups of people at different times. When Covid-19 forced us to work from kitchens and dining tables, it triggered the biggest shift in the workplace in decades. That was just the beginning of a change that will outlive our professional lives. In the coming years, our work world will confront a dynamic array of challenges. Rapid technological advances, as well as the pace of innovation, will demand constant adaptation, posing both opportunities and threats. Global economic uncertainties amplify the need for stronger resilience. The ongoing digital transformation raises concerns about data security and privacy. Climate change awareness requires businesses to navigate sustainability and environmental responsibility. Aspects of inclusion and correcting historical wrongs done over the years will come to the forefront. Remote work dynamics will persist, demanding innovative approaches to team collaboration and employee well-being. Navigating these challenges calls for agile leadership, ethical decision-making and a commitment to continuous innovation in an ever-shifting landscape. Our world of work, the way we work and we who work will all need to change and adapt. As you embark on this journey, remember: the only constant is change, and your ability to shape the narrative about what impacts you will shape the narrative of your professional future.

In one of the Harry Potter books, Firenze the Centaur teaches students a course in divination or predicting the future. He takes a different approach than the students have gotten used to. As one of them puts it: 'His priority did not seem to be to teach them what he knew, but rather to impress upon them that nothing, not even . . . knowledge, was foolproof.'

It is estimated that there are about 3 billion people in the global workforce and more than 300 million companies.[1] Though nowhere in the numbers and scale of the galaxies observed by the Hubble telescope, this still represents a vast universe to be explored. Hidden in this world will be more lessons to be learnt in our quest to make work more human and to be better humans at work.

Acknowledgements

This book has benefited greatly from the learning and wisdom of many people.

Firstly, I would like to thank my family—Geeta and Trisha for their love, patience and support. Trisha spent her Christmas vacation at university helping me with critical comments and edits.

I'm indebted to Mrs Sudha Murty, with whom I first broached the idea of writing a book. She unhesitatingly stated that this is something that I must do and encouraged me throughout.

I would like to thank the incredible team at Penguin Random House India—the wonderful Radhika Marwah who believed that this book was possible and helped me through the process; the editing team comprising Sakshi Sharma who gave brilliant insights and made me think beyond what I had written; and the delightfully competent Yash Daiv who made this book better.

Finally, I want to say thank you to my friends and my colleagues at both Infosys and Tech Mahindra for their encouragement and support.

Notes

Introduction

1 According to Statista, the estimated number of companies worldwide was approximately 333.34 million in 2023.

Chapter 1: Is the Robot Applying for My Job?

1 The World Economic Forum (WEF) Future of Jobs Report of 2023 surveyed more than 800 companies that collectively employ 11.3 million workers across forty-five countries worldwide. Global employers estimate a net loss of 14 million roles. Low-level workers will bear the brunt of the fast-moving changes. AI will cut around 26 million jobs in administrative positions. The study anticipates that the proliferation of AI will significantly disrupt the labour market. However, the WEF believes that the net impact of most technologies will be positive for employment growth over the next five years.

2 Oestergaard, K. (2024, April 18). *Airbus and Boeing report February 2024 commercial aircraft orders and deliveries*. Flight Plan. https://flightplan.forecastinternational.com/2024/03/18/airbus-and-

boeing-report-february-2024-commercial-aircraft-orders-and-deliveries/

3 NHS backlog data analysis. https://www.bma.org.uk/advice-and-support/nhs-delivery-and-workforce/pressures/nhs-backlog-data-analysis

4 *The Future of Jobs Report 2020*. World Economic Forum. (n.d.). https://www.weforum.org/publications/the-future-of-jobs-report-2020/

5 The hotel chain CitizenM uses technology to transform how guests sleep, work and relax. The chain offers smart guest rooms and automated common areas. Arriving travellers are welcomed by an ambassador and can bypass the front desk to check in, using a kiosk or a mobile app. A digital key is created, and guests are on their way in one minute. Technology in the room can enable the guest to configure the environment, interact with others, plan their day and even watch unlimited movies.

6 On 4 June 1981, a National Campaign Committee comprising eight central trade unions and national industrial federations was formed in Mumbai to counter the faulty anti-labour policies of the government. In the all-India conference in Hyderabad in 1984, one of the unions decided to observe 1984 as 'Anti-Computerisation Year' to oppose labour displacing computerization. It was a time when computerization was spreading in the industrial and banking sectors. The union's stand was that instead of assisting labour, it was displacing labour and capturing its place. Their stand was that India needed labour-intensive technology to accommodate the ever-growing army of unemployed people waiting for jobs.

7 World Bank Report 9412-IN India 1991, Country Economic Memorandum August 1991

Chapter 2: Painting a Masterpiece While Clearing Your Mail

1 According to workplace productivity studies conducted by *Economist Impact* in 2023, 42 per cent of office workers surveyed said they are unable to spend more than an hour a day on focused work without encountering distraction.

2 According to Statista, the estimated number of companies worldwide was approximately 333.34 million in 2023.

3 The University of Northern Carolina in 2010 surveyed 182 senior managers across a range of industries to find that 71 per cent of managers think of meetings as unproductive and inefficient; 65 per cent said meetings keep them from completing their own work; and 64 per cent said meetings come at the expense of deep thinking. A study in 2023 by the software company Atlassian reveals that the average employee spends thirty-one hours in unproductive meetings over a month. (Contributor, N. P. A., Paczka, N., & Contributor, C. A. (2023, February 8). *Meetings in the workplace: 2024 statistics*. LiveCareer. https://www.livecareer.com/resources/careers/planning/workplace-meetings-2022-statistics).

4 In a study conducted in 2008 at the University of California, Irvine, it was found that, on an average, individuals require approximately twenty-three minutes and fifteen seconds to regain focus and return to their task after being distracted. (The cost of interrupted

work: More speed and stress. (n.d.-b). https://ics.uci.edu/~gmark/chi08-mark.pdf).

5 Thoreau, Henry D. *Walden: Or, Life in the Woods*. Book on Demand Ltd, 2019.

6 You could use any tool available online. Examples include https://www.psycom.net/internet-addiction-test-quiz or https://psychology-tools.com/test/internet-addiction-assessment Please note that these are just indicative to help you calibrate and are not certified assessments by qualified mental health professionals.

7 Quality management systems first entered the workplace in the 1920s as statistical methods to improve work output. Pioneered by Walter A. Shewhart, an ever-increasing demand for greater and greater productivity saw the need to develop a more robust, structured and logical approach to quality. Key to the development of the total quality management (TQM) techniques that industries still rely on today were pioneers like Joseph Juran and W. Edwards Deming, alongside other thought leaders such as A.V. Feigenbaum, Philip Crosby and Kaoru Ishikawa.

8 The TQM methodology includes the whole company in the pursuit of high quality, especially the workers closest to the job. An example is the quality circle, in which workers directly involved in a process brainstorm to discover solutions. You can see these charts displayed at the workplace, especially in manufacturing facilities.

Chapter 3: Dr Jekyll and Mr Manager

1 New data published in DDI World's Frontline Leader Project in 2019 dives into the emotions and relationships of frontline managers. The survey collected data

from more than 1000 managers, senior leaders and individual contributors. The research continues in the line of results that other similar surveys have shown. The study data shows that 57 per cent of employees have left a job because of their manager. Furthermore, 14 per cent have left multiple jobs because of their managers. An additional 32 per cent have seriously considered leaving because of their manager.

2 A study conducted in 2022 by MIT's Sloan School of Management found that a toxic workplace culture is the number one reason people leave their jobs and is 10.4 times more likely to contribute to attrition than compensation. The authors analysed the impact of more than 170 cultural topics on employee attrition in companies from April through September 2021. (Donald Sull, C. S. (2022, January 11). *Toxic culture is driving the great resignation*. MIT Sloan Management Review. https://sloanreview.mit.edu/article/toxic-culture-is-driving-the-great-resignation/)

3 Snyder, B. (2015, April 2). *Half of us have quit our job because of a bad boss*. Fortune. https://fortune.com/2015/04/02/quit-reasons/

4 *What is psychological safety?*. Harvard Business Review. (2023, February 15). https://hbr.org/2023/02/what-is-psychological-safety

5 Encyclopædia Britannica, inc. (2024, March 9). *The Blitz*. Encyclopædia Britannica. https://www.britannica.com/event/the-Blitz

6 Computer systems technology, including information technology and communications, has some of the worst employers. That's according to a new survey, based on data from Glassdoor (2023). The research looked at data for over 1.3 million companies and, based on

reviews of employers, the tech sector showed up near the bottom of the list for bad bosses.

7 Researchers analysed 1.4 million Glassdoor reviews in 2023 from nearly 600 major US companies and found employees describe toxic workplaces in five main ways: non-inclusive, disrespectful, unethical, cutthroat and abusive. (The five biggest red flags of a toxic culture, according to a study of more than one million Glassdoor reviews | inc.com. (n.d.-b). https://www.inc.com/jessica-stillman/toxic-workplace-culture-mit-study.html).

8 Robert I. Sutton PhD, *The No Asshole Rule: Building a Civilized Workplace and Surviving One That Isn't*, (USA: Business Plus, Reprint edition, 2010).

Chapter 4: Embracing Tomorrow: Rediscovering Health for a Fulfilling Life

1 Maslow, A. H. (2015). *A theory of human motivation*. BN Publishing.

2 The Pomodoro Technique is a time management method developed by Francesco Cirillo in the late 1980s to help him plan his study time as a university student. It uses a kitchen timer to break work into intervals, typically twenty-five minutes in length, separated by short breaks. Each interval is known as a pomodoro, from the Italian word for tomato, after the tomato-shaped kitchen timer Cirillo used.

3 Strong social relationships increase the likelihood of survival by 50 per cent regardless of age, sex or health status, according to a meta-analysis of 148 studies on mortality risk by a team from Brigham Young

University(2010)They found social disconnection is at least as harmful to people as such well-accepted risk factors as obesity, physical inactivity and smoking up to fifteen cigarettes a day. (ScienceDaily. [2010, July 28]. Relationships improve your odds of survival by 50 percent, research finds. ScienceDaily. https://www.sciencedaily.com/releases/2010/07/100727174909.htm).

4 *Friends & Happiness in the Workplace Survey & Stats.* We Are Wildgoose. (n.d.). https://wearewildgoose.com/uk/news/friends-in-the-workplace-survey/

5 Sherry Glied, K. A., Kinder, M., & Pugliese, J. (2016, July 28). *Exercise increases productivity.* Brookings. https://www.brookings.edu/articles/exercise-increases-productivity/

6 Languishing can involve or become clinical depression; not everyone who experiences languishing meets the criteria for depression, and vice versa. Clinical depression is a disorder outlined in the *Diagnostic and Statistical Manual of Mental Disorders*, whereas languishing is not. Mental health professionals would view depression as a clinical diagnosis, while they might view languishing as a failure to thrive.

Chapter 5: Crafting Human Experiences at Work

1 *W. Edwards Deming quote.* A. (n.d.). https://www.azquotes.com/quote/873755

2 Microsoft's latest survey (2023) on business trends compiles input from 2700 employees and 1800 business decision makers in the United States, United Kingdom and Japan across job functions to uncover

the ways technology is, or is not, helping them do their work. The findings show that, while advancements in workplace technology help get more work done, they don't enable employee experience in the same way.

Chapter 6: Imagining Your Office of the Future

1 On 19 October, 1973, following President Nixon's request for Congress to make available $2.2 billion in emergency aid to Israel for the conflict known as the Yom Kippur War, the Organization of Arab Petroleum Exporting Countries (OAPEC) instituted an oil embargo on the United States The embargo ceased U.S. oil imports from participating OAPEC nations, and began a series of production cuts that altered the world price of oil. These cuts nearly quadrupled the price of oil from $2.90 a barrel before the embargo to $11.65 a barrel in January 1974. In March 1974, amid disagreements within OAPEC on how long to continue the punishment, the embargo was officially lifted.

2 A GitHub survey shows that Copilot promises to unlock productivity for everyone. Among developers who use GitHub Copilot, 88 per cent say they are more productive, 74 per cent say that they can focus on more satisfying work and 77 per cent say it helps them spend less time searching for information or examples.

3 The average person at rest takes about sixteen breaths per minute. This means we breathe about 960 breaths an hour, 23,040 breaths a day, 8,409,600 a year.

4 Devices enabled by the Internet of Things (IoT) have become ubiquitous and part of the office. Organizations across manufacturing, retail, healthcare and others employ IoT as part of their critical daily operations

as well. Forrester predicts that the world will reach 1 trillion IoT devices by 2025. This poses a risk to organizations, as once a smart device is hacked, the opportunities for a malicious actor to move laterally to enterprise assets or steal data greatly increase. As bad actors exploit these security gaps and IoT adoption grows, enterprise security emerges as a critical point.

5 American architect Frank Lloyd Wright had a tremendous impact on the architecture and aesthetics of buildings. In the later part of his career, he helped a few set designers of science fiction films show us the future through innovative designs. Among the most iconic examples of his work in science fiction sets is his concept of the flying saucer from the 1951 film *The Day the Earth Stood Still*. In his concept, Wright depicted the flying saucer without doors or windows, where beings can enter as if entering the surface of a living tissue. The surface would then close as if it were healing like a cut in the skin or closing like a wound, leaving behind a continuous surface without a scar. To design the office of the future, we need imagination, simplicity and to always keep the user in mind.

Chapter 7: Failing Successfully

1 Lincoln's failure list reads as follows: Lost job in 1832; defeated for state legislature in 1832; failed in business in 1833; defeated for Speaker in 1838; defeated for nomination for Congress in 1843; elected to Congress in 1846 but lost renomination in 1848; rejected for land officer in 1849; defeated for U.S. Senate in 1854; defeated for nomination for Vice President in 1856 and defeated for U.S. Senate in 1858.

2 What is success by Ralph Waldo Emerson. (n.d.). http://cl.stmarytx.edu/wluo/poem.html

3 The loss of the space shuttle *Challenger* was caused by a failure in the joint between the two lower segments of the right solid rocket motor. The specific failure involved the destruction of the seals designed to prevent hot gases from leaking through the joint during the rocket motor's propellant burn. The decision to launch the Challenger was flawed because the launch date in January was cold, and there was a recommendation from the engineers advising against the launch at temperatures below 53°F. This is an example of a failure with high consequences that could have been avoided. However, learnings from this failure resulted in several changes to the launch process at NASA.

4 Ng, B. (2018, January 26). *The neuroscience of growth mindset and intrinsic motivation*. Brain sciences. https://www.ncbi.nlm.nih.gov/pmc/articles/PMC5836039/

5 Most of us won't remember the Newton—a personal digital assistant developed by Apple computers in the early 1990s. Newton was a device that was ahead of its time in terms of technology and ideas but did not do well due to its price and some product bugs. However, many of its features and ideas were incorporated into the iPad a decade later. The iPad was a runaway success, but Newton's failure helped produce a better design.

Chapter 8: Playing the Long Game

1 The Tour de France is the world's most prestigious and difficult bicycle race. It attracts the world's best riders in a gruelling contest. Staged in July, it typically takes place over twenty days and covers some 3600 kilometres.

The Tour presents cyclists with challenges due to its division into stages that encompass both flat terrain and extensive mountainous inclines. Since it is spread out over many days, the participants must carefully plan their strategy and efforts. It is a rare cyclist who can perform well at every stage. Since the stages involve both time trials and climbing, it requires a lot of planning and cyclists need to capitalize on their strengths while adjusting for their weaknesses to complete the race and win. The one who wins is the one who plays the long game, not worrying about individual stages but focusing on the long-term goal and sticking to their race strategy.

2 The Eastman Kodak Company, a pioneering American photography technology company, began operations in Rochester, New York, in the 1880s. By 1982, Kodak employed around 62,000 people and accounted for half of the area's economic activity. Kodak went into sustained decline once photography became digital. The company filed for bankruptcy in 2012, and by the end of 2016, it employed around 1600 people.

Chapter 9: Doing the Right Things Right

1 The B-737 problems did not end here. A door plug on an Alaska Airlines flight 1282 fell off a few minutes after take-off from Portland International Airport on 5 January 2024. The plane made a safe emergency landing, and no one was seriously injured. An investigation revealed that shoddy manufacturing was the cause.

2 In India, the Whistle Blowers Protection Act, 2014, protects people who bring to notice allegations of

corruption, misuse of power or commission of a criminal offence against a public servant. In the US, section 922 of the Dodd-Frank Wall Street Reform and Consumer Protection Act provides that the Commission shall pay awards to eligible whistle-blowers who voluntarily provide the SEC with original information that leads to a successful enforcement action.

3 In May 2018, Martin Winterkorn, 70, the former chairman of the management board of Volkswagen AG (VW), was charged with conspiracy and fraud. As part of its plea agreement with the US government, VW paid a criminal penalty of $2.8 billion.

4 In 2021, Facebook changed its company name to Meta, reflecting the company's growing ambitions beyond social media.

5 The companies mentioned in this chapter are not chosen with any intent to draw attention or comment on their management or business practices. The incidents quoted are purely meant to serve as illustration of concepts in the chapter and are based on information in the public domain. The author acknowledges the contribution made by these companies over the years to business and innovation through their products and services.

6 The Hippocratic Oath is an ethical oath traditionally taken by physicians. In its original form, the oath requires a new physician to swear by a number of healing gods, to uphold specific ethical standards. The oath is the earliest expression of medical ethics in the western world, establishing several principles. The seminal articulation of principles is the phrase 'First do no harm.' (Latin: *Primum non nocere*). It urges the medical practitioner to promise not to cause any harm to the patient through their intervention.

Epilogue

1 According to Statista, the estimated number of companies worldwide was approximately 333.34 million in 2023.

Scan QR code to access the
Penguin Random House India website